Toe-Up 2-at-a-Time Socks

Toe-Up
2-at-a-Time
Socks

MELISSA MORGAN-OAKES

Photography by John Gruen

Storey Publishing

The mission of Storey Publishing is to serve our customers by
publishing practical information that encourages
personal independence in harmony with the environment.

Edited by Gwen Steege and Kathy Brock
Art direction and book design by Mary Winkelman Velgos
Text production by Liseann Karandisecky

Photography by © John Gruen
Photo styling by Raina Kattelson
How-to illustrations by Alison Kolesar
Charts by Leslie Anne Charles

Indexed by Nancy D. Wood

Storey Publishing
210 MASS MoCA Way
North Adams, MA 01247
www.storey.com

Printed in China by Toppan Leefung Printing Ltd.
10 9 8

LIBRARY OF CONGRESS CATALOGING-IN-PUBLICATION DATA

Morgan-Oakes, Melissa.
  Toe-up 2-at-a-time socks / by Melissa Morgan-Oakes.
    p. cm.
  Includes index.
  ISBN 978-1-60342-533-9 (hardcover with concealed wire-o : alk. paper)
  1. Knitting—Patterns. 2. Socks. I. Title. II. Title: Toe-up-two-at-a-time socks.
TT825.M6663 2010
746.43'2041—dc22
                                2009052447

For Gene,
The other day I was breathing,
you know, in and out, in and out?
And suddenly I realized that
what I was breathing was you.
Thank you.

Contents

Can't Get Away from Those Socks!

As soon as the last word was written
for *2-at-a-Time Socks*, the idea of
a toe-up sock book began to grow
in my mind. I'd made a decision
to stop with socks for a bit, just
a little bit, and knit things that
were not socks, and not two at a
time on one long circular needle.
I sat down with yarn and needles,
and considered what I could create. Within a few minutes and
without fully realizing it, I had
cast on for a pair of toe-up socks,
two at a time, reasoning that they
were not really the same as "regular" socks; after all, they began at
the opposite end of things, right?
Nice try, but in the end what I
had were socks. More socks, still
two at once, still matching when
they're done, just "upside down."
Obviously I wasn't going to get
out of socks that easily.

Not being a fan of the short-
row heel, I played around with
unraveling the heel turn and flap
of a top-down sock in my mind,

and soon came up with my own way of doing things. Now, I am sure that someone out there is doing the same thing I do, and for all I know they've written it down already. There are only so many ways to do a thing, after all. But this is my personal take on a particular knitting technique, and I am, as before, biased in its favor. Like *2-at-a-Time Socks*, this book does reflect my personal preferences in terms of heels, toes, yarns, and such. It's my book, so I get to be biased. The heels in this book are all turned heels with a flap of sorts. I believe that they fit better and are more comfortable than a short-row heel. And as with *2-at-a-Time Socks*, I encourage you to use whatever heel method you prefer. Once you've mastered the technique, it can be applied to just about any sock pattern. Toes to the top, top to the toes: Now you're covered in both directions!

chapter 1

Needles, Yarn, and Other Basics

Since writing the first book, I've been asked a few questions consistently enough that I think I should include the answers to them here. Most of the questions I hear, when not relating to specific patterns in *2-at-a-Time Socks*, are about needles, yarns, yarn substitutions, and sizing. I've also included a bit here about casting on and binding off in ways that are appropriate for toe-up sock knitting. I think it's important for knitters to experiment with different techniques and determine what works for their individual knitting styles. And a word about fit: Fitting toe-up socks is not the same as fitting a top-down sock. Some math is required, but not anything too horrible. Truly, if I can do it, you can too!

The Nicest Needles

Knitting cannot happen without needles. As time has passed, I've been introduced to more and more choices in knitting needles. Metal or wood, firm or flexible cables — ultimately the choice is your own. Here I present my favorites and the reasons why they've won me over.

Addi. As a rule, those of us who love Addi Turbo nickel-plated brass needles really, really love them. They take a beating and remain attached to their cable. The join is good and stable and does not catch the yarn. It is likely that you could run them over and they'd be fine, unless you kinked the older kind of cable — then you had a problem. Not any more! Addi has replaced its old steel wire cable with new flexible plastic cables. My new favorites are Addi Natura needles, made of bamboo, which combine the comforting nature of wood with a flexible cable and the same high-quality components as the Turbos. The smallest size currently available is a US size 2, but I live in hope. My next favorites are my beloved slick Addi Turbos, available in sizes beginning with US 000. And after these come the Addi clear-coated brass lace needles (also starting in a size US 000), which have a sharp point that is perfect for lacework on shawls (or socks). With three types of circular needles to choose from, Addi offers options for every project. I am very hopeful that Addi's new Clicks will expand to include interchangeable tips of all three types, and smaller sizes. Addi needles are still, in my opinion, the best way to go.

Inox. I discovered these aluminum needles with their flexible black cable sometime between finishing up the first book and its actual release date. By the time the book came out, I was using the Inox fixed circular needles more and more. They are less expensive than Addis, to be sure, which is important for many of us. After all, inexpensive, good-quality tools mean more money to spend on yarn! The needle itself holds onto the yarn a bit more than Addi Turbos do, so if you have issues with stitches that run away, these are a great alternative.

ADDI TURBO

ADDI NATURA

INOX

Lantern Moon. I love Lantern Moon's straight needles. So does my daughter's big, yellow cat, which chews on them at a disproportionate rate compared to other wooden needles in the house. The cat knows quality when he tastes it. ("Way to be, Mel," the knitter said, sighing.) The company's commitment to traditional crafts, fair trade, and environmental sustainability only adds to the value of the needles, in my opinion. I bought some of their Destiny circulars to try for a sweater project, and ended up using them for some test socks for this book. The needles themselves are wonderful: smooth as butter. The join is not quite as smooth as an Addi join, and the cable is not as flexible as the Addi or Knit Picks cable. Although I have not experienced this, I heard that at one time there had been a problem with the wooden needle coming out of the metal base, but Lantern Moon has corrected this. If you love the feel of wooden needles in your hand (is there someone who doesn't?) these needles are an excellent choice. And I think every knitter should own at least one pair of straight needles, which should be kept away from family pets. As of this writing, their circulars are available in sizes from US 3 to 17, and are a won-

derful thing to have around for knitting thick, warm, worsted- or DK-weight socks!

Knit Picks Harmony.

A few years ago, Knit Picks introduced nickel-plated Options needles. I love the cable, but I "push" my needle when moving stitches around, so the supersharp point of the metal needles wasn't working for me. Then one day I opened a catalog and it was as if the company had read my mind. They had kept the flexible purple cable from the original nickel-plated circulars, but brought in a more organic feeling to the needles, something less cold and certainly less pointy. Enter Options Harmony wood fixed circulars. Great name, too, for the harmonious blend of features in these needles. In the 40-inch length, they're available from 2.0 mm to 3.0 mm in 0.25 mm increments, which give those of us who knit with little needles and skinny yarn a wider range of options when trying to establish the correct gauge for a project. I ordered a bunch of fixed circulars and sat down to swatch. The cable is lightweight and very difficult to kink. It doesn't want to have its own way constantly, and is willing to allow the knitter to work unhindered by staying

LANTERN MOON
DESTINY

SUSANNE
EBONY

mostly out of the way. The join is smooth. I have not yet broken a needle (although I know folks who have), but in the smaller sizes, I would think that it would be only a matter of time before a needle snapped. Fortunately, Knit Picks is very responsive in replacing broken needles quickly.

Kollage Yarns Square Circulars. New to my sphere are these unique needles from Kollage Yarns. Yes, you read that right, it says "square circulars"! The needles themselves are square rather than round. And here's the best part for many of you: The cable goes right past flexible all the way to floppy. I found when working with these needles that their square shape was very comfortable for my fingers, and the flexible cable made it much less likely that ladders would form on my socks. There was a bit of fiddling to get stitches on and off of the cable, though: Because the cable is so relaxed, the stitches are perfectly happy to remain there. A little bit of learning on my part had them coming on and off of the needles more easily. This needle would be a really good choice for anyone who has consistent issues with laddering, as long as that knitter is aware that she needs to allow

time for learning how to manage stitches around the join where needle and cable meet.

The Yummiest Yarns

In my first book, *2-at-a-Time Socks*, all of the featured yarns were machine washable, and most were machine dryable as well. That's changed a bit this time. There are just so many options available to knitters of socks. Wool, silk, mohair, Tencel, cotton, SeaCell — the list seems endless. I even designed a pair of cashmere socks for Judith Durant's *Luxury One-Skein Wonders*. Yes, cashmere, and yes, for socks. Feet deserve yarn-love, too!

Although most of the yarns featured in this book are still machine washable, some are not. The reason? It's pretty simple: I ran an uncontrolled and tremendously unscientific experiment. I knitted a pair of socks and said to my husband, "These don't go in the washer." I should point out here that he does the laundry in our home, and that he has a soft spot for his hand-knit socks. I don't know how this division of labor happened really, except that when we met, I was a full-time student and single mother and he was a single dad with a full-time job. When we combined households and began splitting up chores he jumped on laundry as quickly as I jumped on dishes and cooking. I enjoy doing dishes, and I love to cook. Laundry is a multistep process: place in washer, remove, hang to dry, remove from line, fold, put away. There are a lot of steps, and I think it offends my attention-deficit tendencies. I get lost somewhere between "place in washer" and "put away," and then we're all searching for underwear on a Monday morning, only to discover that they're still in the washer, where they've been since Saturday morning.

But I digress. Where was I? Yes. He took laundry. I reasoned that if he could manage to keep a pair of hand-wash socks intact for a year, then anyone could do it. Not that he's in any way laundry challenged, but keeping track of one pair of socks for a whole year is a lot to ask of a busy man with a crazy wife. Well, he did it. The socks have not once been accidentally stuck in a pant leg, nor have they sneaked into the washer when his back was turned. And yes, he wears them. The truth is that many of these yarns are too irresistible not to knit and wear. They beg for

knitting, and who am I to stand in their way? All they ask is a tiny bit of extra care, and I think we can give them that. But if the thought of a hand-wash-only sock still makes your head hurt, then by all means use a super-wash yarn. There are certainly enough of them to fit your needs.

Yarn Substitutes

This brings us to yarn substitu-tion — how, when, and why? Let's start with when and why. One great "why" is stated above. Perhaps you, like many, don't like the idea of a hand-wash yarn. Maybe the yarn in ques-tion isn't available at your local yarn shop, or maybe you are allergic to the fiber. Possibly the yarn I used in the pattern doesn't come in your preferred color, or maybe you just plain old don't like that yarn and can't figure out why I'd be so crazy as to use it! Some of my sample knitters have had this very reaction. (Don't worry — the objectionable yarns are not in the book!) Regardless of your reason, be it one of those given above or another all your own, give yourself permission to substitute yarn. Don't let an adherence to the yarn featured in any pattern anywhere prevent you from knitting a particular

WORKING THE SWATCH

All joking aside, a swatch truly is an essential piece of information for any knitter. Here are my rules for a perfect gauge swatch:

* Cast on enough stitches to make a swatch at least 4 inches wide. Six inches is even better.
* Knit in garter stitch for a few rows — an inch is ideal.
* Change to stockinette stitch, and knit for 4 inches, keeping the first and last 4 to 6 stitches in garter stitch.
* Work another inch of garter stitch, and bind off.
* Wash and block your swatch. (This allows for any "blooming" as fibers relax that may occur when the yarn is exposed to soap and water.)
* Measure gauge in the stockinette area in the middle of the swatch.

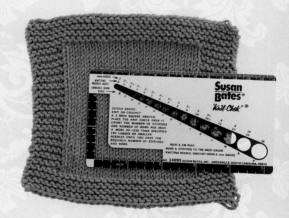

Now I know that very few of us have the patience to knit a swatch like that for a sock. But just keep in mind that gauge is critical in fitting a garment, even a sock. If you don't check gauge, and the sock doesn't fit anyone but the draft horse down the road, well, next time you'll swatch!

item, be it one of my socks or an adorable sweater in a magazine.

Get the gauge. But how do you substitute? How do you know what's safest and best? The first issue you would need to confront, and the most vital, is that of gauge. Let's say the recommended or featured yarn was knitted at a gauge of 8 stitches per inch. In order to substitute a different yarn you must be certain that it will knit at 8 stitches to the inch to make a fabric that is comfortable and pleasing to the eye. You are not, I hope, going to try to knit a pair of socks the book has shown in the lightweight Socks That Rock yarn from Blue Moon Fiber Arts with Cascade 220, which is a worsted-weight yarn. Reading the ball band will give you a good idea of gauge. As a general rule of thumb, most yarns within a given weight range should be roughly interchangeable: fingering for fingering, worsted for worsted, and so on. However, as yarns can vary in gauge, it's very important that you swatch to be sure. You need to knit a swatch anyway, right? Of course you do!

Find the fiber. The next issue to consider in substituting yarn is the fiber content and type

of the original yarn. If the pattern was knitted in a textured, tweedy yarn, the appearance will not be the same if you substitute a smooth, shiny yarn. If the pattern used a fluffy mohair yarn, then it won't look at all similar if you substitute a glossy cotton yarn, and so on. You don't need to run out and find a yarn that looks exactly the same; you merely need to be aware that changing the type of yarn changes the appearance of the sock. You as the knitter then get to take responsibility for that choice, which puts you in the driver's seat! Maybe you think my choice is a bad one and you'd like to see a particular pattern knitted in something completely different. More power to you! Go for it! In fact, it makes me so happy to see people take my ideas and run with them. Just recently I saw a woman wearing a sweater I designed, but she'd added a twist. She had taken the cable pattern used on the body and centered it on the sleeves in a most intriguing manner. I loved it. "Why," I thought, "didn't *I* think of that?" So take my ideas and run with them, please. Change it up at your discretion!

Select the reason. Your yarn choice may be dictated by a wearer's desires, by seasonality,

USING REINFORCING THREAD

Reinforcing thread (or reinforcing yarn) is sometimes used in the heels and toes of socks to increase the longevity and durability of the finished product. Simply hold the reinforcing thread together with your working yarn and knit with the two held together.

or by intended use. For example, I love wool socks pretty much all year long. Not everyone does. I might knit cotton or cotton-blend socks for summer if I am knitting for a friend or family member. Maybe I am considering a pair of fancy socks for formal occasions. In that case I might look for something that has some shiny bits in it (Kraemer Sterling, perhaps?) or something that has a dressy hand and appearance, like Valley Yarns Colrain Lace or Great Adirondack Silky Sock. Hiking socks for me? Well, rugged, toothy wool, of course. On the other hand, if I am knitting hiking socks for someone who cannot abide rugged wool yarn, I might make their hiking socks in softer, machine-washable, worsted-weight wool and use a reinforcing yarn for heels and toes, or possibly for the whole foot. Which brings us to the topic of reinforcing threads.

Reinforce — Really?

Once you've chosen a yarn, it's time to consider whether to use a reinforcing thread for heels and toes. Some of this decision making should involve the personal traits of the wearer. If you know that the intended wearer's commercial socks wear through at the

toe and heel with some rapidity, then I'd add a little something to protect your time and yarn investment. Generally most yarn intended for sock knitting contains some degree of nylon or bamboo to provide strength and durability, and reinforcing threads for average wearers of these yarns are not usually needed. Yarns that require hand washing are more likely to benefit from a reinforcing thread.

As a general rule of thumb, the softer and finer the fiber, the more likely a reinforcing thread is of benefit. Examples include alpaca, cashmere, and merino. When in doubt, err on the side of caution. The extra investment is worth the peace of mind. I like to limit the use of reinforcing thread to toes and heels, although some people find great benefit from using it for the entire foot. If no sock-specific reinforcing threads are available near you, it's possible to use nylon thread such as YLI Corporation's Woolly Nylon, which is available in 55 colors including a good range of neutrals and some variegated shades. This is a thread used in sergers (also known as overlock sewing machines), and it comes on a large but relatively inexpensive cone of 1,000 yards. A few cones in basic colors will likely last a very long time, and if you've got a serger so much the better.

Cast Ons and Bind Offs

There are a few different ways that you can cast on and bind off when knitting toe-up socks.

Casting On

My favorite cast on for toe-up socks (and the only one we're featuring in this book) is Judy's Magic Cast On, created by Judy Becker and used here with her gracious permission. I initially used the figure-eight (or Turkish) cast on, but I never fell fully in love. I discovered Judy's by chance, and it has become my hard-and-fast favorite for toe-up socks, as well as for top-down mittens. Having used various other methods over the years, I can tell you that this takes the proverbial cake. With a bit of practice, it is easily mastered, and well worth the effort! Full directions for Judy's Magic Cast On begin on page 22.

Binding Off

The basic bind off perfectly meets the needs of many knitters, but for others, the basic bind off may prove to be too tight. Two alternative bind offs are presented in the appendix: the sewn bind off and the tubular bind off (see page 159). Both are actually "sewn" bind offs, because they utilize a seaming needle threaded with a long yarn tail.

Another alternative for creating a looser bind off is to increase one stitch between each stitch on the last round of your sock, and then bind off. This will double the number of stitches and create a more comfortable sock. It can make a bit of a ripple, some might even say ruffle. Even though this ripple is not apparent when the sock is on, it may not be right for every application. It also may be possible to bind off using a larger needle, or to simply remember to keep your stitches very loose when binding off. You'll want to experiment to determine which is best for your knitting style. You can make swatches and practice binding off. The swatches do not need to be very large, just enough to bind off stitches and check for flexibility in the bound-off edge of the piece. You could also consider practicing these bind offs on larger shapes. Practice does not have to produce things you cannot use. With a little ingenuity your practice pieces can become holiday ornaments, tea cozies, pillow covers, or cell-phone cases!

Adapting Toe-Up 2-at-a-Time Socks

As with *2-at-a-Time Socks*, this technique can be easily adapted to nearly any sock pattern. It's easiest if the pattern you're adapting has an even number of stitches. This way you can simply "split" the sock in half the same way the patterns in this book are designed. Half of the stitches will be side 1, or the instep side.

The other half will be side 2, or the sole (and eventually heel) stitches.

One of the most-asked questions I receive is about changing a sock pattern to fit a foot when the eventual wearer has a foot that is smaller or larger than that stated in the pattern. We as knitters can find ways to make size adjustments in our patterns. We can change gauge, add or subtract pattern repeats, or draft a pattern entirely of our own design. Changing gauge is probably the simplest way to adjust a size. Let's say you want to knit a particular pattern for your sister who has a very narrow foot. The finished circumference of the sock as written is 8 inches. But her skinny little foot only measures 7 inches around. If you used a smaller needle and got, for example, 8 stitches to the inch rather than the stated gauge of 7 stitches to the inch, you could follow the directions as written and your finished sock would measure close to 7 inches around.

This book gives a finished foot circumference for every sock pattern in both sizes. When deciding which size to knit, consider that the finished sock should be smaller in circumference than the foot of the wearer.

Most of the stitch patterns in this book create a sock with a fair amount of stretch.

All of the patterns in this book require you to know the desired foot length. This can be based on shoe-size conversion charts (see page 164), or it can be based on the actual measurement of a foot from heel to toe. The best way to measure is the old-fashioned way. Stand, or have your intended victim — oops, *recipient* — stand on a piece of white paper and draw around the foot with a pencil.

After you have the foot measurement, you need to perform a basic mathematical calculation using a simple formula that determines how long your gusset and heel turn will be, based on your row gauge (see Toe-Up Math, page 19). Use these numbers to calculate how long you knit the foot of your sock before beginning gusset increases.

Now you're armed with knowledge and ready to enter the world of knitting socks two at a time on one long circular needle from your toes on up. Time to cast on and get to work!

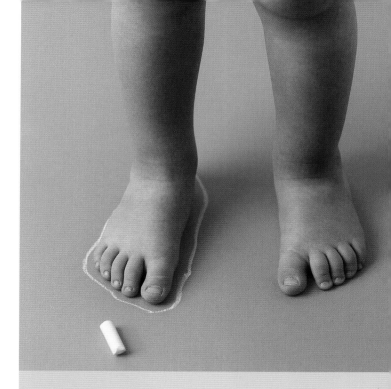

SENTIMENTAL STEPS

When I size socks for a child by tracing his or her foot, I like to date the outline. As the child grows, I can place his or her foot back on the same paper, matching heel to heel, and draw a new "growth ring," adding a date each time. This piece of paper is exceptionally sniffle-worthy for grandmothers, mothers, and high-quality aunts. You can sit and remember the tiny feet that now fill the page from end to end. If needed, a second sheet of paper can be taped onto the end of the first, extending the space available. These pages can be kept in a loose-leaf binder or a simple paper folder along with other pertinent knitterly info: how long were Johnny's arms, what was his girth, how long was his back neck measurement on the same date, and so on. (See, I do knit more than socks!) Add on some information about favorite colors and styles, and you're set for more than a year's worth of knitted gifts in the case of a child (or longer for an adult).

chapter 2

Step-
by-Step
2-at-a-Time

In spite of repeated efforts to stop knitting socks,
I find myself unable to do so. Socks, for now, are my
life. I design and knit other things too, but socks
pretty much rule me.

    That's a great reason to knit any sock, but
there are more reasons to go toe-up. As in my first
book, *2-at-a-Time Socks,* both socks are started and
completed at the same time, which means they're
basically identical. I can cast on and bind off both
at one time. By beginning socks at the toe, you can
also try them on as you knit them. This ensures
that they fit you, or their intended wearer, very
well. We can all go to the store and buy socks that
fit, or most of us can. I have a pretty small foot for
a woman, and commercially made women's socks
are a little big for me. Kids' socks are made for kids.
(Nothing against kids, but I really don't like their
socks.) If I knit my own, my socks always fit. Most
significantly, toe-up socks mean that I can begin my
socks with a questionable amount of yarn and just

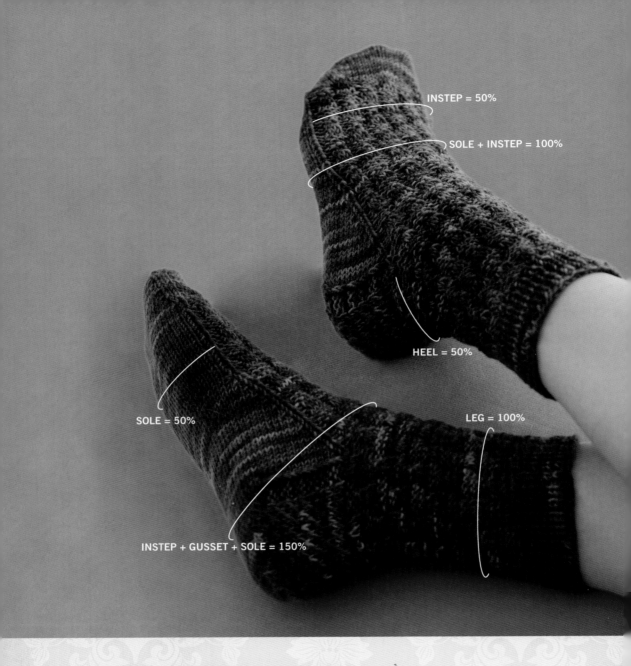

INSTEP = 50%

SOLE + INSTEP = 100%

HEEL = 50%

SOLE = 50%

LEG = 100%

INSTEP + GUSSET + SOLE = 150%

A MATTER OF PERCENTAGE

As with top-down socks, you can think of toe-up socks in terms of percentages. After toe increases, the total number of stitches around the foot for each sock equals 100 percent. Instep stitches are generally 50 percent. Soles and heels are usually worked on the other 50 percent. When gussets are added, the total percentage increases to 150 percent. As the heels are created, the number of stitches decreases. The goal is to return to 100 percent as the heel is completed. Using this information, you can adapt any sock pattern to your particular style.

stop when I run out. That could mean leftovers from a previous project to make socks for a child, or ankle socks for me. I can knit with partial skeins until I've got a few yards left, and then bind off my identical socks.

Toe-Up Sock Anatomy

Toe-up socks "my way" differ from top-down socks only in the direction of the knitting. Beginning with a small number of cast-on stitches, increases form the toe. The foot is then knitted for a bit, until it's time to increase for the gussets (the triangular areas on either side of the heel). Determining how long to knit the foot requires a little bit of math (explained below), but it's well worth it. Once the gusset has been created, it's time to make a cup for the heel to sit in. Short rows give the heel a rounded shape. Next, more short rows effectively eat up the added gusset stitches while a heel flap is built. Then it's back to working in the round on the leg.

Toe-Up Math

The key to the proper fit of a toe-up sock is knowing when to start the gusset increases on the foot.

Here's what you need to know:
1 The desired length of finished sock. This can be obtained from a shoe-size conversion chart (see page 164) or by measuring the foot of the intended wearer (see Adapting Toe-Up 2-at-a-Time Socks on page 14).
2 The number of rows it will take to build the gussets and the heel cup. This number varies depending on the particular pattern and size of sock that you are knitting. To make it easy for you, I have already calculated this number and provided it in each of the patterns in this book.
3 Your row gauge. Rows per inch varies depending on the pattern, knitter, yarn, and needle, so I can't just give you this number (see sidebar at right). However, you can easily determine it by counting the number of rows in 1 inch. Measure along one column of stockinette stitch on the sole side after you've completed a couple of inches of the foot.

Plug the above three pieces of information into the easy mathematical formula on page 20 (and with individual patterns) to calculate the length of foot before you begin the gusset increases— "toe-to-gusset length."

WHY CAN'T I JUST GIVE YOU NUMBERS?

Row gauge can vary between knitters even when stitch gauge is the same. Some people disagree with me. If you don't agree, try this simple experiment. Set five or six knitters down with the same yarn and a few different sizes of needle. Knit until everyone is getting a given stitch gauge, asking them to change needles as needed to meet gauge. After they've knitted a few inches at proper *stitch* gauge, stop and measure everyone's *row* gauge. My guess is the row gauges will vary.

Now, do this in reverse. Knit until everyone is getting a stated *row* gauge. After a few inches, check everyone's *stitch* gauge. I bet they are not all getting the same number of stitches per inch. This explains why I can't give you the numbers. You've got to get them yourself!

Let's take the pattern for Ballet (page 98) as an example.

❶ **The desired length** of finished sock. For me this is a blissfully short 8¼ inches.

❷ **The number of rows** it will take to build the gusset and the heel cup; for the small size of Ballet, this is 53.

❸ **My row gauge.** Measured vertically along the stockinette portion of the sole of my sock, this is 11 rows per inch.

When I apply the formula (see box below), I find that I should knit the feet until the socks measure approximately 3.45 inches from the tips of the toes to the needle. Although you can round this measurement a little, it's best to round down. Socks stretch, and so shorter is generally better than longer. (Metric users can just substitute centimeters for inches.)

TOE-TO-GUSSET FORMULA

X = your desired total sock length
Y = number of rows in gusset and heel cup
Z = your rows per inch, measured on the sole of sock
TGL = toe-to-gusset length

$$X - (Y \div Z) = TGL$$

Here is my completed formula for figuring the measurement from toe to the beginning of the gusset increases for Ballet in size Small (pp. 98–105).

X (my desired total sock length)	= 8.25"
Y (number of rows in gusset and heel cup)	= 53
Z (my rows per inch, measured on the sole of sock)	= 11
TGL (toe-to-gusset length)	= 3.43"

$$8.25" - (53 \div 11) = 3.43"$$
$$X \quad - (\ Y \ \div \ Z\ ) = TGL$$

Sample Toe-Up Socks

I'll demonstrate the 2-at-a-time toe-up technique using a worsted-weight yarn in two colors to make it easier to follow along. If you knit these sample socks at a gauge that's comfortable for you, they should fit a child about two to four years old.

Needles. To get started with your toe-up 2-at-a-time socks, you need a 40" (100 cm) circular needle. I used a US size 5 (3.75 mm), but I knit loosely and you may find it easier to work with a larger needle. Because these are sample socks, getting gauge is not as important as the learning!

Markers. You will need several stitch markers to knit these socks. I recommend a locking stitch marker, because you can easily attach it to the work. A scrap of contrasting-color yarn tied to the work also serves the purpose.

Yarn. You also need about 60 yards each of two different colors of a worsted-weight yarn. The yarn I used for the sample socks is Valley Yarns Valley Superwash, but any worsted-weight yarn will work. The gauge for the actual sample socks is around 6 stitches per inch, although as I said above gauge is not critical here. (This may be the only time you ever hear me say those words! Gauge is always critical in garment construction.)

Knitting the Sample Socks

Let's get started! Knitting two socks at one time from the toes up is simple once you understand the techniques involved. By following along with the step-by-step instructions below, you'll be knocking out socks in perfect pairs in no time!

In this section, I give the pattern instructions for the sample socks first along with a photo, often followed by an explanation of exactly how to carry out those instructions. As you knit other patterns in the book, you can easily refer back to this section for explanations and visuals whenever you get "stuck."

JUDY'S MAGIC CAST ON FOR 2-AT-A-TIME SOCKS

The cast-on technique shown here is an adaptation of Judy's Magic Cast On (© Judy Becker 2006). It shows how to cast two sets of stitches (one for each sock) onto one long circular needle: Half the total number of stitches for each sock are cast on to each half of the circular needle. These stitches become the very tips of the toes of your socks. Next, you knit one round to properly seat those stitches on your needle.

QUICK-START MATERIALS LIST

To build your own pair of sample socks, all you need are a 40" circular needle, yarn, and some stitch markers. Here's what we used to create the sample you'll be knitting:

NEEDLE	US 6 (4.0 mm) 40" (100 cm) circular needle or whatever needle size is comfortable with your yarn
YARN	60 yards (55 m) each of two colors of worsted-weight yarn. (For the sample socks, I recommend using a different color yarn for sock B and sock A, so you can distinguish them more easily. I used Valley Yarns Valley Superwash in Teal for sock B and Misty Lilac for sock A.)
NOTIONS	One split-ring or locking stitch marker and two regular stitch markers
ABBREVIATIONS	K Knit P Purl M1R Make 1 right (see Backward Loop Increases, page 159) M1L Make 1 left (see Backward Loop Increases, page 159)

Casting On Stitches for Sock B

1 **Set Up** Using the yarn for sock B, make a slip knot, leaving a tail of about 14" (35.5 cm). Place the loop around one of the needles. This anchor loop counts as the first stitch.

✳ *Once you master this cast on, you may want to try starting with just a loop of yarn on the top needle in place of the slip knot. Just be sure the tail end hangs down the side of the needle that is away from you. This results in a smoother toe, without the little bump that the slip knot leaves.*

ANCHOR LOOP ON TOP NEEDLE.

2 Hold both needles together in your right hand with their tips pointing to the left. The needle holding the anchor loop should be on top and the empty needle should be on the bottom. Make sure both strands of yarn hanging down from the anchor loop are positioned on the side of the bottom needle that is away from you. Hold the yarn in your left hand so that the tail goes over your index finger and the working yarn (the yarn that leads to the ball) goes over your thumb.

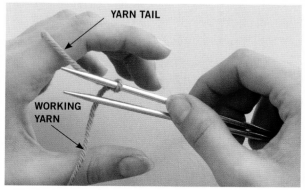

YARN TAIL OVER INDEX FINGER AND WORKING YARN OVER THUMB.

✳ *I've found that it can be tricky not to default to the long-tail cast on when learning this method. Remember that the yarn tail goes over your finger, not over your thumb.*

3 **Bottom Needle**
Make a loop on the bottom needle by moving the yarn tail on your finger below the bottom needle (A), up around the bottom needle, and then down between the two needles (B). Pull the loop snug around the needle.

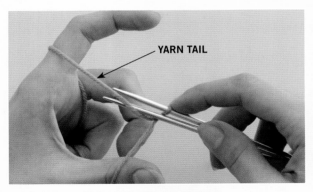

(A) YARN TAIL BELOW THE BOTTOM NEEDLE.

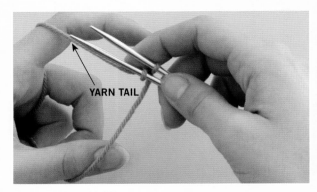

(B) MAKING THE LOOP.

4 **Top Needle** Make a loop on the top needle by moving the working yarn on your thumb away from you, up around the top needle, and down between both needles. Pull the loop snug around the needle.

❈ *Note that the top yarn strand always wraps around the bottom needle, and the bottom yarn strand always wraps around the top needle. Just remember: "Top around bottom, bottom around top."*

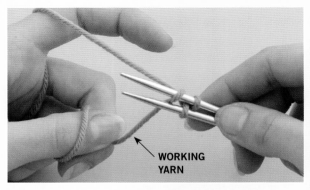

TWO STITCHES ON TOP NEEDLE: THE CAST-ON STITCH AND THE ANCHOR LOOP.

5 Continue to alternately cast a stitch on to the bottom needle and then the top needle, as shown above in steps 3 and 4, until you have cast on the desired number of stitches for sock B. The sample sock has 16 stitches cast on: 8 stitches on the top needle and 8 stitches on the bottom needle.

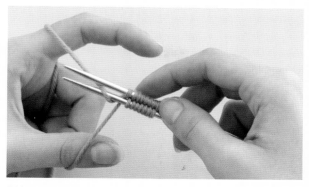

CASTING ON THE FINAL STITCH FOR SOCK B.

✳ *Check that your last stitch was cast on to the bottom needle using the yarn tail. If not, you may have made two consecutive loops on the same needle, or you may have used the same yarn strand to make loops on both needles. Carefully check your cast on stitches for irregularities. When checking that you have cast on the correct number of stitches for your sock, be sure to count the stitches on both halves of the circular needle. Also, remember that the anchor loop counts as the first stitch.*

✳ *On the side of your work facing you, the stitches should look like two rows of offset loops. On the opposite side (which will become the inside of the toe), you'll see a row of twists that look like purl bumps.*

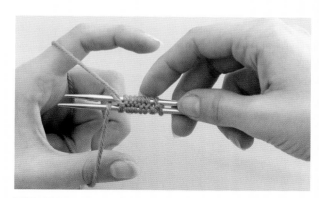

PURL BUMPS ON THE OPPOSITE SIDE OF YOUR WORK.

Casting On Stitches for Sock A

(6) Drop the yarn for sock B and push the cast-on stitches farther onto the needles. Using the yarn for sock A, repeat the Casting On Stitches for Sock B section (steps 1–5 above) to cast on the stitches for the next sock onto the same circular needle.

✳ *The sample socks have 16 stitches cast on for each sock: 8 stitches on the top needle and 8 stitches on the bottom needle.*

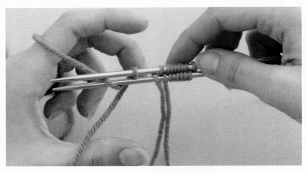

CASTING ON THE FIRST STITCHES FOR SOCK A.

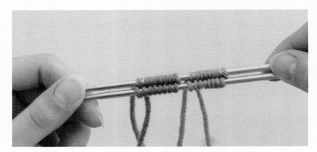

ALL STITCHES CAST ON FOR SOCK A (LILAC) AND SOCK B (TEAL).

(7) Rotate your work clockwise so that both needle tips are pointed to the right and the side of your work without the bumps is still facing you. Next, trim your yarn tails to about 6" (15 cm) so that you don't accidentally knit with them. Take care not to cut your working yarn.

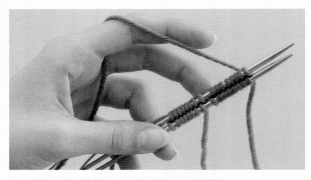

ALL STITCHES CAST ON AND WORK ROTATED.

✳ *The stitches currently on the top of your work are referred to as "side 1" because they are worked first at the start of each round; they will become the insteps (tops of the feet) of your socks. The stitches on the bottom needle are called "side 2"; they will become the soles of your socks.*

Knitting Round 1

8 **Side 1, Sock A**
With the needle tips pointed to the right and the smooth side of the work facing you, pull the bottom needle to the right until the stitches lie on the cable (A).

✳ *When you empty the bottom needle to prepare to knit side 1, all the side 2 stitches lie on the cable.*

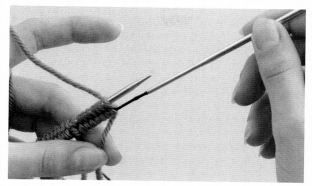

(A) PULL THE BOTTOM NEEDLE TO THE RIGHT.

9 Position the yarn tail and the working yarn for sock A so they hang straight down from your work and are not crossed. Then, move the yarn tail straight back away from you and to the left so it goes behind the working yarn. It should pass between the working yarn and the top needle (B).

✳ *Be certain to "lock" your yarn tail in place behind the working yarn. This is important, because it ensures that your final cast-on stitch is held closed.*

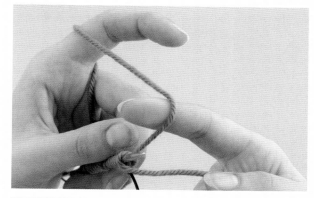

(B) YARN TAIL IN PLACE UNDER WORKING STRAND.

10 Knit the first stitch of side 1, sock A onto the empty needle.

✳ *The first stitch will probably loosen as you knit it. Pull gently on the tail to snug it back up.*

11 Attach a locking or split-ring stitch marker into this first knit stitch to indicate the beginning of your rounds. (You might find it easier to do this on the first stitch of Round 2.)

KNITTING THE FIRST STITCH.

✳ *It is important to position this marker so it goes into the stitch, not around the needle. It remains in place in that stitch until your socks are complete.*

12 Knit to the end of side 1, sock A. You are now in position to move to side 1, sock B.

✳ *Look at the stitches that you have just worked for sock A. They should appear as stockinette stitches.*

SIDE 1, SOCK A STITCHES COMPLETE.

(13) Side 1, Sock B
Drop yarn A and pick up yarn B. Repeat steps 9–12 above to knit side 1, sock B, remembering to lock in the tail as described above.

✳ *With side 1 of both socks complete, you are ready to rotate your work.*

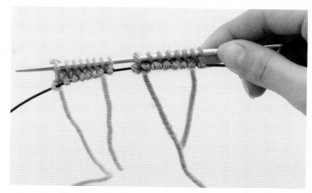

SIDE 1, OF SOCK B (TEAL) AND SOCK A (LILAC) COMPLETE.

(14) Side 2, Sock B
Rotate your work clockwise so that the working yarn for sock B is on the right and the stitches on the cable are on the top. Push the top needle to the left so that the stitches on the top half of the cable move onto that needle and are ready to be knit. Pull the bottom needle to the right so that the stitches you just knit lie along the bottom half of the cable.

Knit through the back loops of the stitches on side 2, sock B. (See page 161 of the Glossary if you need a refresher on how to knit through the back loop.)

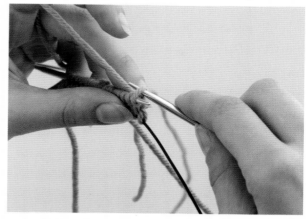

✳ *It is important that you knit through the back loops here, because this particular cast on twists the stitches that you cast on for side 2. To untwist them, you knit them through the back loops on the first round only.*

KNITTING THROUGH THE BACK LOOPS ON SIDE 2.

✳ *Look at the stitches you just worked and check that they appear as stockinette stitches. If you see a row of purl bumps here, you may have been working on the inside of side 1, rather than continuing in the round to work the outside of side 2.*

(15) **Side 2, Sock A**
Drop yarn B and pick up yarn A. As on sock B, knit through the back loops of the stitches on side 2, sock A.

When this first round is complete, you now have what appears to be two rows of stockinette stitches for each sock. These stitches will become the very tip of the toes of your socks.

---

(16) Rotate your work so that the tips of the needles point to the right and the stockinette side of the work is facing you. Push the top needle to the left so that the side 1 stitches for both socks are ready to be knit from it. Pull the bottom needle to the right so that the stitches for side 2 of both socks lie along the cable. You should be back at your marker, indicating that you have reached the end of the round.

✳ *Note: If you didn't place a marker into the first stitch on Round 1, then do so now.*

Congratulations! You've just successfully cast on and worked the first round of your socks. You are now ready to begin Round 2. *If you are making the sample socks,* continue to Shaping the Toes and step 17 on the page. *If you are knitting one of the project socks,* return to your sock pattern to proceed.

Shaping the Toes

For increasing on the toes of these socks, I prefer a backward loop increase. I think it's easier to knit into on the next round than other types of increases. By looping the yarn in different directions you can create either a right-leaning or left-leaning version of this increase (referred to as M1R and M1L). Using these different versions of the increase on opposite sides of a sock gives a more uniform appearance to the two sides. (For instructions on how to make an M1R and M1L increase, see page 159.)

17 **Round 2 (increase)**
SIDE 1, **sock A:** K1, M1R, knit to one stitch before the end of side 1 of sock A, M1L, K1.

SIDE 1, **sock B:** Drop yarn A; pick up yarn B. K1, M1R, knit to 1 stitch before the end of side 1 of sock B, M1L, K1.

INCREASES COMPLETED ON SIDE 1 OF BOTH SOCKS.

18 **Rotate** Rotate your work and arrange your stitches on the needles (as you did previously) so that you are ready to work the sole stitches on side 2 of the socks.

SIDE 2 (SOLE), **sock B:** K1, M1R, knit to 1 stitch before the end of side 2 of sock B, M1L, K1.

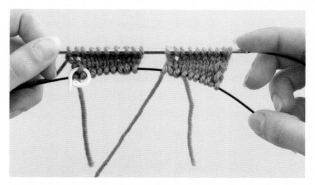

INCREASES COMPLETED ON BOTH SIDES OF BOTH SOCKS.

SIDE 2 (SOLE), **sock A:** Drop yarn B; pick up yarn A. K1, M1R, knit to 1 stitch before the end of side 2 of sock A, M1L, K1.

✳ *You've just completed the first increase round of socks A and B. Each sock now has 20 stitches (10 stitches on each side of each sock).*

19 **Rotate** Rotate work and arrange stitches so that you are ready to begin Round 3.

20 **Round 3 (even)** Knit every stitch on each side of each sock without any increases, remembering to change yarn when switching from sock to sock. Note: One complete round includes working the following sections: side 1 of sock A, side 1 of sock B, side 2 of sock B, side 2 of sock A (in that order). When you end each round, you'll be back at the marker.

21 **Next Rounds** Repeat Rounds 2 and 3 three more times, increasing in one round (steps 17–19 above), then knitting the next round even (without increases, step 20) until each sock has 32 stitches (16 stitches on each side of each sock).

TOE INCREASES COMPLETED.

✻ *Phew! Your toes are done. Now you can move on to the feet of your sample socks.*

Knitting the Feet

To knit the feet, you work in the round on both socks, without any more increases, until your socks are a certain length. For the sample socks, I specify this length. However, as you'll see, each pattern in this book includes an easy formula for calculating this measurement for custom-fitting socks.

22 **All Rounds** Knit all rounds (stockinette stitch) until socks measure 2" (5 cm) from beginning of toes. End your work having just finished side 2 of sock A. You are now back at your marker at the beginning of side 1 of sock A, ready to begin the gusset increases.

FEET OF BOTH SOCKS COMPLETE.

Increasing for the Gussets

Gussets widen the foot of the sock to accommodate your heel; they are the part of the sock where the foot transitions into the leg. When the foot is long enough, you create the gussets by working increases on both sides of the sole stitches only. You increase on alternate rounds until you reach the specified number of gusset stitches for your socks.

23 **Round 1 (increase)**
SIDE 1 (INSTEP),
socks A and B: Work in stockinette stitch as established.

SIDE 2 (SOLE), socks B and A: K1, M1R, knit to last stitch of each sock, M1L, K1.

 These increases are made only on the sole (side 2) of the socks.

FIRST ROUND OF GUSSET INCREASES COMPLETED.

24 **Round 2 (even)** Knit every stitch on each side of each sock without any increases.

25 **Next Rounds**
Repeat Rounds 1 and 2 (steps 23 and 24 above) seven more times. End having just worked Round 2.

SIDE 1 (INSTEP) of each sock still has 16 stitches.

SIDE 2 (SOLE) of each sock now has 32 stitches.

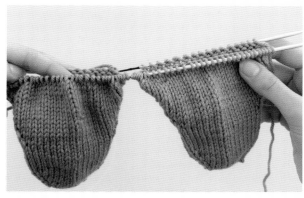

GUSSET INCREASES COMPLETE.

TIPS FOR SHAPING THE HEEL

A heel cup is the rounded shape at the bottom of the heel of a sock. In the patterns in this book, the heel cups are shaped by working "short rows." The short-row technique is used to add length to a certain section of knitting. On these rows, you work only part way across, and then turn and work back across the same stitches. To shape the heel cup, you work back and forth on the center stitches, working 2 fewer stitches on each row until you are left with a given number of stitches in the center of the heel. To avoid holes at the turns, you wrap a stitch at each turn and then knit (or purl) the wraps together with their stitches on the first two rows after you've completed the heel cup.

To avoid potential confusion, I use the terms "right side" and "wrong side" (rather than "front" and "back") to indicate how to move your yarn as you create the wrap. The "right side" is the side that will eventually be displayed to the public (usually the knit side). The "wrong side" is the side that will be against your skin (usually the purl side). Front and back may be relative, but most of us know right from wrong!

NOTE: Because you use short rows on both the heel cup and heel flap, these sections are worked separately: You first work side 2 of sock B back and forth in rows to the completion of the heel cup and heel flap, then you work side 2 of sock A in a similar manner. At the completion of the heels, you return to knitting the socks together in rounds.

Shaping the Heel Cups

26 **Set Up** This is a partial round, worked only on side 1 (instep) of both socks (see Tips for Shaping the Heel, at left).

SIDE 1 (INSTEP), socks A and B: Knit to the end. Rotate work and arrange stitches so that you are ready to begin working the heel on side 2 of sock B.

27 SIDE 2, **sock B,** Row 1 (right side) K8, place marker 1 (A), K15, slip 1 as if to purl (B), bring yarn to right side to wrap stitch, place marker 2 on left-hand needle (C), slip stitch back to left-hand needle. Turn work to the wrong side.

✳ *The stitches between the markers become your heel cup. The stitches on the outside of the markers are gusset stitches, which will be worked later. From this point on, the heel cup is worked back and forth in rows on side 2 (sole) of sock B.*

A

B

C

FIRST RIGHT-SIDE ROW IS COMPLETE.

28 SIDE 2, **sock B,** Row 2 (wrong side) Bring yarn to wrong side of work, putting it into position to purl (A). Purl to 2 stitches before marker 1, slip 1 as if to purl (B), bring yarn to right side to wrap stitch, slip stitch back to left-hand needle. Turn work to right side (C).

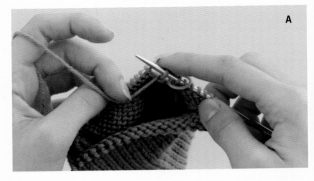

FIRST WRONG-SIDE SHORT ROW IS COMPLETE.

(29) SIDE 2, **sock B,** Row 3 (right side) Bring yarn to wrong side of work (in position to knit) (A). Knit to 2 stitches before previously wrapped stitch (B), slip 1 as if to purl, bring yarn to right side to wrap stitch, slip stitch back to left-hand needle. Turn work.

KNIT ACROSS THE RIGHT SIDE TO TWO STITCHES BEFORE PREVIOUSLY WRAPPED STITCH.

(30) SIDE 2, **sock B,** Row 4 (wrong side) Bring yarn to wrong side of work (in position to purl). Purl to 2 stitches before previously wrapped stitch (it's helpful to look on the right side to identify the wrapped stitch). Slip 1 as if to purl, bring yarn to right side to wrap stitch, slip stitch back to left-hand needle. Turn work.

PURL ACROSS THE WRONG SIDE TO TWO STITCHES BEFORE PREVIOUSLY WRAPPED STITCH.

31 **Next Rows** Repeat
Rows 3 and 4 until all but
the 3 center stitches have been
wrapped. End having just completed a right-side row. Turn work.

✳ *Now that the heel cup of sock B is
complete, you will move on to building
the heel flap of this sock. You will work
the heel cup and flap of sock A after you
have completed the heel of sock B. You
are now ready to work the heel flap.
Note: The other sock patterns in this
book have different numbers of stitches
left unwrapped at the center of the heel.*

HEEL CUP FOR ONE SOCK COMPLETED AND WORK TURNED.

TIPS FOR WORKING WRAPPED STITCHES

A heel flap is the part of the sock that wraps around the back of your heel.
In the patterns in this book, you create heel flaps by working back and forth
in short rows on the center heel cup stitches while "eating up" the gusset
stitches on either side. Each short row creates a gap between the edge of the
heel flap and the gusset stitches. This gap is closed by working the stitches
at the edge of the heel flap together with a stitch from the gusset. This
gradually decreases the number of stitches down to the number needed for
knitting the leg.

In this section you will lift the wraps you just created and knit (or purl)
them together with their respective stitches. You can distinguish the wrapped
stitches from regular stitches because they're wearing a little "noose" around
their necks. When you work each stitch together with its wrap, you move the
noose and hide it behind the stitch it was wrapped around. The completed
wrap should not be visible on the right side of the fabric. You may be able to
lift the wraps and knit into the stitch in one step, but most knitters like to
use the tip of the right-hand needle to lift the wrap up onto the left-hand
needle, and then knit or purl the two together in a way that hides the wrap.
(For more information, see Working Wrapped Stitches, page 162.)

Working the Heel Flap

In this section you will work back and forth in rows on side 2 (sole) of sock B.

32 SIDE 2, **sock B,** Row 1 (wrong side) Purl, lifting wraps and purling them together with their respective stitches as you come to them, to 1 stitch before marker 1 (see Tips for Working Wrapped Stitches, at left). Slip 1 as if to purl, remove marker, slip stitch back to left-hand needle, and purl the next 2 stitches together (P2tog). Turn.

PURLING 2 STITCHES TOGETHER TO BEGIN HEEL FLAP.

33 SIDE 2, **sock B,** Row 2 (right side) Slip 1 as if to purl. Then knit, lifting the wraps and knitting them together with their respective stitches as you come to them, to 1 stitch before marker 2. Lift the wrap of the next stitch completely over and to the left of the stitch (A); slip the stitch as if to knit, slip the wrap as if to knit, remove marker (B), slip next stitch as if to knit, place the 2 slipped stitches and the wrap back on left-hand needle, and knit the 2 slipped stitches together with the wrap through the back loop (C). Turn.

KNITTING THE 2 SLIPPED STITCHES TOGETHER WITH THE WRAP THROUGH THE BACK LOOP.

(34) **SIDE 2, sock B,** Row 3 (wrong side) Slip 1 as if to purl, purl to 1 stitch before gap, P2tog to close gap. Turn.

✳ *Note the gap that is present between the first or last stitch of your heel flap and the next stitch of the gusset.*

GAP BETWEEN HEEL FLAP AND GUSSET ON WRONG SIDE.

(35) **SIDE 2, sock B,** Row 4 (right side) Slip 1 as if to purl, *K1, slip 1 as if to purl; repeat from * to 1 stitch before gap, ssk to close gap. Turn.

GAP BETWEEN HEEL FLAP AND GUSSET ON RIGHT SIDE.

(36) **Next Rows** Repeat Rows 3 and 4 until you have worked all of the stitches on side 2 of sock B. End having completed a right-side row. You now have 16 stitches on side 2 of sock B. You are now ready to work the heel cup and heel flap of sock A.

SOCK B HEEL COMPLETED.

Sock A Heel Cup and Heel Flap

Repeat all rows in the Sock B heel cup and heel flap sections (steps 27–36 above) for side 2 of sock A.

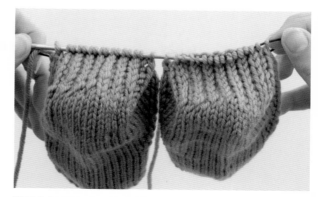

HEELS COMPLETED ON BOTH SOCKS.

Knitting the Legs

Now that the heels are complete, you are ready to begin working the leg and cuff of the socks. You will return to working in the round for both socks. A hole can form at the point where the heel and instep meet. The set-up round below addresses this problem.

Set Up SIDE 1, **socks A and B:** Pick up a stitch where the heel stitches of sock A meet the instep stitches of sock A. Slip the picked-up stitch back to the left needle and knit it together with the first instep stitch. Knit to 1 stitch before the end of side 1 of sock A. Slip the next stitch as to knit to the right needle. Pick up another stitch

PICKING UP A STITCH WHERE THE HEEL AND INSTEP MEET.

where the instep stitches of sock A meet the heel stitches of sock A. Slip the picked-up stitch and the next stitch back to the left-hand needle and knit them together through the back loop. Repeat for sock B.

SIDE 2, **socks B and A:** Knit across all stitches of both socks.

39 **Leg** Knit every stitch (stockinette stitch) on both sides of both socks A and B until the leg measures 3" (7.5 cm) from the top of the heel flap.

LEGS MEASURING 3 INCHES.

40 **Ribbing** Work K1, P1 rib for 1½" (3.75 cm).

Finishing

41 Bind off all stitches loosely (see Bind Offs, page 159). Weave in tails.

You'll find a number of suggested bind offs on page 159. I recommend that you experiment with different bind offs and find the one that's best suited to your knitting style. It's important that your bind off be flexible and not too tight. Socks work best when you can get your feet into them!

Now that you've completed your sample socks, it's time to try your hand at a pattern on the pages that follow. Enjoy!

chapter 3

Toe-Up
2-at-a-Time
Patterns

It makes me happy when the ideas that hatch in my head
emerge as pretty things people can knit. The patterns in
this book are just that: a collection of lovely, knittable,
wearable socks. The socks range in difficulty from simple
to complex, from a delicately feminine, twisted-stitch
pattern to more straightforward designs to please even
the most selective wearer. There are lots of amazing yarns
here as well. You will find the captivating colors of hand-
dyed and hand-painted yarn; the softness of fine merino,
cotton, and silk; the durability of wool; and even a little
shimmer in the form of a hint of sterling silver. Cables,
lace, and knit-and-purl combinations — I hope there's
something here to intrigue just about everyone. There are
patterns for adults and children, each presented in two
sizes. Whether you choose the angular lines of The Keep
or the intricate grace of Ballet, I hope that you enjoy knitting the patterns presented here for yourself, your family,
and your friends.

Kid Stuff

I love knitting for kids! These are very simple socks in delightful colors hand dyed by Gail Callahan, the Kangaroo Dyer, exclusively for Valley Yarns' Franklin sock yarn. They will knit up fast and be loved by their owners when finished. In the smaller size there's more than enough yarn to knit a third sock, for the one that always ends up lost! You could knit up a whole wardrobe of socks with just a couple skeins of yarn. I've shown two versions of this sock. The smaller one is ribbed on the leg, and the larger is ribbed at the cuff with a stockinette stitch leg.

CHILD'S SIZES	SMALL	LARGE
FINISHED FOOT CIRCUMFERENCE	5¼" (13.5 cm)	7" (18 cm)
YARN	Valley Yarns Franklin, 75% superwash wool/25% nylon, 4 oz (113 g)/450 yds (411 m) [*Yarn band gauge: 7–8 stitches = 1" (2.5 cm) in stockinette stitch on US 0–2 (2.0–2.75 mm) needles*]; Jade (for Small) or Mountain Spring (for Large): 1 skein	
GAUGE	9 stitches and 11 rows = 1" (2.5 cm) in stockinette stitch	
NEEDLE	US 1 (2.25 mm) 40" (100 cm) circular, *or size needed to obtain correct gauge*	
NOTIONS	3 stitch markers (including 1 locking stitch marker), darning needle	

Pattern Stitches

Stockinette
Knit every round.

Ribbing
K2, P2.

Casting On and Shaping the Toes

Cast On Follow the instructions for casting on stitches on pages 23–26 to cast on 12 stitches for sock B and 12 stitches for sock A.

Round 1 Follow the instructions for knitting Round 1 on pages 27–30 to knit the first round on both socks. You now have 6 stitches on side 1 (instep) for each sock and 6 stitches on side 2 (sole) for each sock.

Round 2 (increase)

> **NOTE** All make 1 (M1) increases should be worked with a backward loop increase (see Backward Loop Increases on page 159).

- **SIDE 1 (INSTEP), sock A:** K1, M1R, knit to 1 stitch before the end, M1L, K1.
- **SIDE 1 (INSTEP), sock B:** K1, M1R, knit to 1 stitch before the end, M1L, K1.
- **ROTATE:** Rotate your work and arrange your stitches on the needles so that you are ready to work the sole stitches on side 2 of both socks.
- **SIDE 2 (SOLE), socks B and A:** Repeat the side 1 increases on both socks.
- Each sock now has 16 stitches (8 on each side of each sock).
- **ROTATE:** Rotate your work and arrange stitches so that you are ready to begin the next round.

Next Rounds
- Work Round 2 increases   Ⓢ 3 more times   Ⓛ 5 more times
- Each sock now has   Ⓢ 28 sts   Ⓛ 36 sts

Next Round (even) Knit both sides of socks A and B with no increases.

Next Round (increase) Repeat Round 2.

Next Rounds
- Repeat the last 2 rounds (knit even and increase)
                                                Ⓢ 4 more times   Ⓛ 6 more times
- End your work back at the marker having just finished side 2, sock A.
- Each sock now has a total of   Ⓢ 48 sts   Ⓛ 64 sts
- Each side of each sock now has   Ⓢ 24 sts   Ⓛ 32 sts

Knitting the Feet

Round 1

- SIDE 1 (INSTEP), **socks A and B:** Work in stockinette stitch on all stitches.
- SIDE 2 (SOLE), **socks B and A:** Knit to end (stockinette stitch).

Next Rounds Repeat the previous round, continuing to work in stockinette stitch on sides 1 and 2 of both socks, until the socks measure the appropriate length (see Toe-to-Gusset Length, at right). End your work having just finished side 2, sock A. You are back at your marker and ready to begin the gusset increases.

> ### TOE-TO-GUSSET LENGTH
>
> Use this handy formula. Note: For Z, measure on side 2 of sock.
>
> | | | |
> |---|---|---|
> | **X** (desired total sock length) | = | _____ " |
> | **Y** (# of rows in gusset and heel cup) | = 35 (S); 47 (L) |
> | **Z** (rows per inch) | = _____ |
> | **TGL** (toe-to-gusset length) | = _____ " |
>
> $$\underline{\hspace{1cm}}" - (\underline{\hspace{1cm}} \div \underline{\hspace{1cm}}) = \underline{\hspace{1cm}}"$$
> $$\qquad X \qquad\quad Y \qquad Z \qquad\quad TGL$$
>
> For more information, see Toe-Up Math, page 19.

Increasing for the Gussets

Round 1 (increase)

- SIDE 1 (INSTEP), **socks A and B:** Continue to work in stockinette stitch as established.
- SIDE 2 (SOLE), **socks B and A:** K1, M1R, knit to last stitch of each sock, M1L, K1.

Round 2 (even)

- SIDE 1 (INSTEP), **socks A and B:** Continue to work in stockinette stitch as established.
- SIDE 2 (SOLE), **socks B and A:** Work in stockinette stitch as established.

Next Rounds

	S	L
• Repeat Rounds 1 and 2	**S** 11 more times	**L** 15 more times
• Side 1 (instep) of each sock still has	**S** 24 sts	**L** 32 sts
• Side 2 (sole) of each sock now has	**S** 48 sts	**L** 64 sts

Shaping the Heel Cup, Sock B

Set Up This is a partial round, worked only on side 1 (instep) of both socks.
- **SIDE 1 (INSTEP), socks A and B:** Work in stockinette stitch as established.
- **ROTATE:** Rotate work and arrange stitches so that you are ready to begin working the heel on side 2 of sock B.

> **NOTE** While shaping the heel cup and working the heel flap, you temporarily switch to working the socks individually. You first work side 2 of sock B back and forth in short rows, then you work side 2 of sock A in a similar manner. When the heels are completed, you return to knitting the socks together in rounds (in the Knitting the Legs section). For information about short rows and wrapping stitches, see Tips for Shaping the Heel (page 34).

Side 2, Row 1 (right side)
- Knit   S 12 sts   L 16 sts
- Place marker 1.
- Knit   S 23 sts   L 31 sts
- Slip 1 as if to purl, bring yarn to the right side to wrap stitch, place marker 2 on left-hand needle, slip stitch back to left-hand needle. Turn work to the wrong side.

Side 2, Row 2 (wrong side)
Purl to 1 stitch before marker 1, slip 1 as if to purl, bring yarn to right side to wrap stitch, slip stitch back to left-hand needle. Turn work to the right side.

Side 2, Row 3 (right side)
Knit to 2 stitches before previously wrapped stitch, slip 1 as if to purl, bring yarn to right side to wrap stitch, slip stitch back to left-hand needle. Turn.

Side 2, Row 4 (wrong side)
Purl to 2 stitches before previously wrapped stitch, slip 1 as if to purl, bring yarn to right side to wrap stitch, slip stitch back to left-hand needle. Turn.

Next Rows Repeat Rows 3 and 4 until all but the 4 center stitches have been wrapped. End having just completed Row 3.

Working the Heel Flap, Sock B

NOTE Continue to work back and forth in rows on side 2, sock B only. During the first two rows of the heel flap, you will be lifting and working the wraps that you created in the heel-cup shaping steps above. For information on lifting and working wraps on the right and wrong side, see Tips for Working Wrapped Stitches (page 38).

Side 2, Row 1 (wrong side) Purl, lifting the wraps and purling them together with their respective stitches as you come to them, to 1 stitch before marker 1. Then, lift the wrap of the stitch before marker 1, slip both stitch and wrap to the right-hand needle as if to purl, remove marker, slip both stitch and wrap back to the left-hand needle, and purl together the wrap and its stitch along with the next stitch (P3tog). Turn.

Side 2, Row 2 (right side) Slip 1 as if to purl. Then knit, lifting the wraps and knitting them together with their respective stitches as you come to them, to 1 stitch before marker 2. Lift the wrap of the next stitch completely over and to the left of the stitch, slip the stitch as if to knit, slip the wrap as if to knit, remove marker, slip next stitch as if to knit, place the 2 slipped stitches and the wrap back on left-hand needle, and knit the 2 slipped stitches together with the wrap through the back loop. Turn.

Side 2, Row 3 (wrong side) Slip 1 as if to purl, purl to 1 stitch before gap, P2tog to close gap. Turn.

Side 2, Row 4 (right side) Slip 1 as if to purl, *K1, slip 1 as if to purl; repeat from * to 1 stitch before gap, ssk to close gap. Turn.

Side 2, Row 5 (wrong side) Slip 1 as if to purl, purl to 1 stitch before gap, P2tog to close gap. Turn.

Next Rows Repeat Rows 4 and 5 until you have decreased away all of the gusset stitches on side 2 of this sock. End having completed a right-side row.

  • Side 2 of sock B now again has   S 24 sts   L 32 sts

Shaping the Heel Cup and Working the Heel Flap, Sock A

To shape the heel cup and work the heel flap of sock A, repeat the instructions for sock B above.

Knitting the Legs

In this section you return to working in the round on all stitches for both socks.

NOTE Pick up an extra stitch at the point where the heel and instep meet to prevent holes from developing. (See Knitting the Legs, pages 41–42.)

For Child's Small only

Next Rounds Work in the round in K2, P2 rib on all stitches on both socks A and B until the measurement from the top of the heel flap is 3" (7.5 cm).

Go to Finishing.

For Child's Large Only

Next Rounds Work in stockinette stitch on all stitches for both socks until the measurement from the top of the heel flap is 2" (5 cm).

Next Rounds Work in K2, P2 rib on all stitches on both socks A and B until the ribbing measures 2" (5 cm).

Go to Finishing.

Finishing

Loosely bind off all stitches using your preferred method (see Bind Offs, pages 159–160). Weave in loose tails. Block.

Soft Waves

This is a great sock to wear in cooler weather, when toes beg for extra warmth. Living in New England, I can heartily appreciate good thick socks! Knitted in a heavier weight yarn, these socks will knit up quickly. The simple design will please just about everyone.

ADULT'S SIZES	SMALL	LARGE
FINISHED FOOT CIRCUMFERENCE	6½" (16.5 cm)	8¾" (22 cm)
YARN	Blue Moon Fiber Arts Socks that Rock Heavyweight, 100% superwash merino, 7 oz (198 g)/350 yds (320 m) [Yarn band gauge: 6 stitches = 1" (2.5 cm) on US 3–4 (3.25–3.5 mm) needles]; Lunasea: 1 skein	
GAUGE	5 stitches and 7½ rows = 1" (2.5 cm) in stockinette stitch	
NEEDLE	US 5 (3.75 mm) 40" (100 cm) circular, or size needed to obtain correct gauge	
NOTIONS	3 stitch markers (including 1 locking stitch marker), cable needle, darning needle	

Pattern Stitches

Stockinette
Knit every round.

Ribbing
*K1,P1; repeat from *.

Soft Waves (multiple of 6)
See the Soft Waves Chart on page 59.
Round 1: *P1, K1, slip 1 to cable needle and hold in back, K1, K1 from cable needle, K1, P1; repeat from *.
Round 2: *P1, K1, slip 1 to cable needle and hold in front, K1, K1 from cable needle, K1, P1; repeat from *.

Casting On and Shaping the Toes

Cast On Follow the instructions for casting on stitches on pages 23–26 to cast on 8 stitches for sock B and 8 stitches for sock A.

Round 1 Follow the instructions for knitting Round 1 on pages 27–30 to knit the first round on both socks. You now have 4 stitches on side 1 (instep) for each sock and 4 stitches on side 2 (sole) for each sock.

Round 2 (increase)

> **NOTE** All make 1 (M1) increases should be worked with a backward loop increase (see Backward Loop Increases on page 159).

- **SIDE 1 (INSTEP), sock A:** K1, M1R, knit to 1 stitch before the end, M1L, K1.
- **SIDE 1 (INSTEP), sock B:** K1, M1R, knit to 1 stitch before the end, M1L, K1.
- **ROTATE:** Rotate your work and arrange your stitches on the needles so that you are ready to work the sole stitches on side 2 of both socks.
- **SIDE 2 (SOLE), socks B and A:** Repeat the side 1 increases on both socks.
- Each sock now has 12 stitches (6 on each side of each sock).
- **ROTATE:** Rotate your work and arrange stitches so that you are ready to begin the next round.

Next Rounds
- Work Round 2 increases   **S** 2 more times   **L** 4 more times
- Each sock now has   **S** 20 sts   **L** 28 sts

Next Round (even) Knit both sides of socks A and B with no increases.

Next Round (increase) Repeat Round 2.

Next Rounds
- Repeat the last 2 rounds (knit even and increase)
  S 3 more times   **L** 4 more times
- End your work back at the marker having just finished side 2, sock A.
- Each sock now has a total of   **S** 36 sts   **L** 48 sts
- Each side of each sock now has **S** 18 sts   **L** 24 sts

Knitting the Feet

Round 1
- **SIDE 1** (INSTEP), **socks A and B:** Work the Soft Waves Chart, beginning at the lower right.
- **SIDE 2** (SOLE), **socks B and A:** Knit to end (stockinette stitch).

Next Rounds Repeat the previous round, continuing to work the Soft Waves Chart on side 1 of each sock and keeping side 2 in stockinette, until the socks measure the appropriate length (see Toe-to-Gusset Length, at right). End your work having just finished side 2, sock A. You are back at your marker and ready to begin the gusset increases.

TOE-TO-GUSSET LENGTH

Use this handy formula. Note: For Z, measure on side of sock.

X	(desired total sock length)	=	_____ "
Y	(# of rows in gusset and heel cup)	= 27 (S); 35 ◖
Z	(rows per inch)	=	_____
TGL	(toe-to-gusset length)	=	_____ "

$$\underline{}" - (\underline{} \div \underline{}) = \underline{}"$$
$$\quad\ \ \text{X}\qquad\quad \text{Y}\qquad \text{Z}\qquad\ \text{TGL}$$

For more information, see Toe-Up Math, page 19.

Increasing for the Gussets

Round 1 (increase)
- **SIDE 1** (INSTEP), **socks A and B:** Continue to work the Soft Waves Chart as established.
- **SIDE 2** (SOLE), **socks B and A:** K1, M1R, knit to last stitch of each sock, M1L, K1.

Round 2 (even)
- **SIDE 1** (INSTEP), **socks A and B:** Continue to work the Soft Waves Chart as established.
- **SIDE 2** (SOLE), **socks B and A:** Work in stockinette stitch as established.

Next Rounds
- Repeat Rounds 1 and 2   Ⓢ 8 more times   Ⓛ 11 more times
- Side 1 (instep) of each sock still has   Ⓢ 18 sts   Ⓛ 24 sts
- Side 2 (sole) of each sock now has   Ⓢ 36 sts   Ⓛ 48 sts

S Small   L Large

Shaping the Heel Cup, Sock B

Set Up This is a partial round, worked only on side 1 (instep) of both socks.
- **SIDE 1 (INSTEP), socks A and B:** Work the Soft Waves Chart as established.
- **ROTATE:** Rotate work and arrange stitches so that you are ready to begin working the heel on side 2 of sock B.

NOTE While shaping the heel cup and working the heel flap, you temporarily switch to working the socks individually. You first work side 2 of sock B back and forth in short rows, then you work side 2 of sock A in a similar manner. When the heels are completed, you return to knitting the socks together in rounds (in the Knitting the Legs section below). For information about short rows and wrapping stitches, see Tips for Shaping the Heel (page 34).

Side 2, Row 1 (right side)
- Knit   S 9 sts   L 12 sts
- Place marker 1.
- Knit   S 17 sts   L 23 sts
- Slip 1 as if to purl, bring yarn to the right side to wrap stitch, place marker 2 on left-hand needle, slip stitch back to left-hand needle. Turn work to the wrong side.

Side 2, Row 2 (wrong side) Purl to 1 stitch before marker 1, slip 1 as if to purl, bring yarn to right side to wrap stitch, slip stitch back to left-hand needle. Turn work to the right side.

Side 2, Row 3 (right side) Knit to 2 stitches before previously wrapped stitch, slip 1 as if to purl, bring yarn to right side to wrap stitch, slip stitch back to left-hand needle. Turn.

Side 2, Row 4 (wrong side) Purl to 2 stitches before previously wrapped stitch, slip 1 as if to purl, bring yarn to right side to wrap stitch, slip stitch back to left-hand needle. Turn.

Next Rows Repeat Rows 3 and 4 until all but the 4 center stitches have been wrapped. End having just completed   S Row 4   L Row 3

For Adult's Small Only

Next Row Knit 3 stitches, slip 1 as if to purl, bring yarn to right side to wrap stitch, slip stitch back to left-hand needle. Turn.

Working the Heel Flap, Sock B

NOTE Continue to work back and forth in rows on side 2, sock B only. During the first two rows of the heel flap, you will be lifting and working the wraps that you created in the heel-cup shaping steps above. For information on lifting and working wraps on the right and wrong side, see Tips for Working Wrapped Stitches (page 38).

Side 2, Row 1 (wrong side) Purl, lifting the wraps and purling them together with their respective stitches as you come to them, to 1 stitch before marker 1. Then, lift the wrap of the stitch before marker 1, slip both stitch and wrap to the right-hand needle as if to purl, remove marker, slip both stitch and wrap back to the left-hand needle, and purl together the wrap and its stitch along with the next stitch (P3tog). Turn.

Side 2, Row 2 (right side) Slip 1 as if to purl. Then knit, lifting the wraps and knitting them together with their respective stitches as you come to them, to 1 stitch before marker 2. Lift the wrap of the next stitch completely over and to the left of the stitch, slip the stitch as if to knit, slip the wrap as if to knit, remove marker, slip next stitch as if to knit, place the 2 slipped stitches and the wrap back on left-hand needle, and knit the 2 slipped stitches together with the wrap through the back loop. Turn.

Side 2, Row 3 (wrong side) Slip 1 as if to purl, purl to 1 stitch before gap, P2tog to close gap. Turn.

Side 2, Row 4 (right side) Slip 1 as if to purl, *K1, slip 1 as if to purl; repeat from * to 1 stitch before gap, ssk to close gap. Turn.

Side 2, Row 5 (wrong side) Slip 1 as if to purl, purl to 1 stitch before gap, P2tog to close gap. Turn.

Next Rows Repeat Rows 4 and 5 until you have decreased away all of the gusset stitches on side 2 of this sock. End having completed a right-side row.
  • Side 2 of sock B now again has   S 18 sts   L 24 sts

Shaping the Heel Cup and Working the Heel Flap, Sock A

To shape the heel cup and work the heel flap of sock A, repeat the instructions for sock B above.

Knitting the Legs

In this section you return to working in the round on all stitches for both socks.

NOTE Pick up an extra stitch at the point where the heel and instep meet to prevent holes from developing. (See Knitting the Legs, pages 41–42.)

Next Round

- SIDE 1 (INSTEP), **socks A and B:** Work across instep stitches according to the Soft Waves Chart as established.
- SIDE 2 (SOLE), **socks B and A:** Work these stitches according to the Soft Waves Chart, following the same row in the chart that you used on side 1.

Next Rounds Continue working in the round, following the Soft Waves Chart for all stitches, until the leg measurement from the top of the heel flap is

S 5½" (14 cm)   L 6" (15 cm)

Next Rounds Work K1, P1 ribbing on all stitches for 1" (2.5 cm).

Finishing

Loosely bind off all stitches using your preferred method (see Bind Offs, pages 159–160). Weave in loose tails. Block.

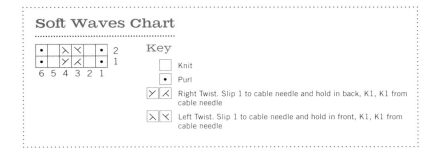

Soft Waves Chart

Key

- Knit
- Purl
- Right Twist. Slip 1 to cable needle and hold in back, K1, K1 from cable needle
- Left Twist. Slip 1 to cable needle and hold in front, K1, K1 from cable needle

Tuscany

This stitch pattern creates a dimpled surface that really brings out the depth and richness of hand-painted yarns. Although any color could be used, I particularly love the soft green, bright blue, and rich red and gold of Lorna's Laces Tuscany. The foot is worked in plain stockinette stitch, and the pattern stitch is reserved just for the leg. Note that the pattern stitch creates a snug fit on the leg of this sock.

WOMAN'S SIZES	SMALL	LARGE
FINISHED FOOT CIRCUMFERENCE	7½" (19 cm)	9" (23 cm)
YARN	Lorna's Laces Shepherd Sock, 80% superwash wool/20% nylon, 2 oz (57 g)/215 yds (197 m) [*Yarn band gauge: 7 stitches = 1" (2.5 cm) in stockinette stitch on US 1 (2.25 mm) needles*]; Tuscany: 2 skeins	
GAUGE	8 stitches and 11 rows = 1" (2.5 cm) in stockinette stitch	
NEEDLE	US 1 (2.25 mm) 40" (100 cm) circular, *or size needed to obtain correct gauge*	
NOTIONS	3 stitch markers (including 1 locking stitch marker), darning needle	

Pattern Stitches

Stockinette
Knit every round.

Ribbing
*K1,P1; repeat from *.

Tuscany (multiple of 6)
See the Tuscany Chart on page 66.
Rounds 1–4: *K3, slip 3 stitches as if to purl wyib; repeat from *.
Round 5: *K3, yo, slip next 2 stitches together as if to knit, K1, pass 2 slipped stitches over the knit stitch, yo; repeat from *.
Round 6: Knit.
Rounds 7–10: *Slip 3 stitches as if to purl wyib, K3; repeat from *.
Round 11: *Yo, slip next 2 stitches together as if to knit, K1, pass 2 slipped stitches over the knit stitch, yo, K3; repeat from *.
Round 12: Knit.

Casting On and Shaping the Toes

Cast On　Follow the instructions for casting on stitches on pages 23–26 to cast on 16 stitches for sock B and 16 stitches for sock A.

Round　Follow the instructions for knitting Round 1 on pages 27–30 to knit the first round on both socks. You now have 8 stitches on side 1 (instep) for each sock and 8 stitches on side 2 (sole) for each sock.

Round 2 (increase)

> **NOTE** All make 1 (M1) increases should be worked with a backward loop increase (see Backward Loop Increases on page 159).

- **SIDE 1 (INSTEP), sock A:** K1, M1R, knit to 1 stitch before the end, M1L, K1.
- **SIDE 1 (INSTEP), sock B:** K1, M1R, knit to 1 stitch before the end, M1L, K1.
- **ROTATE:** Rotate your work and arrange your stitches on the needles so that you are ready to work the sole stitches on side 2 of both socks.
- **SIDE 2 (SOLE), socks B and A:** Repeat the side 1 increases on both socks.
- Each sock now has 20 stitches (10 on each side of each sock).
- **ROTATE:** Rotate your work and arrange stitches so that you are ready to begin the next round.

Next Rounds

- Work Round 2 increases　　　　　S 5 more times　　　L 6 more times
- Each sock now has　　　　　　　S 40 sts　　　　　　L 44 sts

Next Round (even)　Knit both sides of socks A and B with no increases.

Next Round (increase)　Repeat Round 2.

Next Rounds

- Repeat the last 2 rounds (knit even and increase)

  　　　　　　　　　　　　　　S 4 more times　　　L 6 more times
- End your work back at the marker having just finished side 2, sock A.
- Each sock now has a total of　　　S 60 sts　　　　L 72 sts
- Each side of each sock now has　　S 30 sts　　　　L 36 sts

Knitting the Feet

Round 1
- **SIDE 1 (INSTEP), socks A and B:** Work in stockinette stitch on all stitches.
- **SIDE 2 (SOLE), socks B and A:** Knit to end (stockinette stitch).

Next Rounds Repeat the previous round, continuing to work in stockinette stitch on sides 1 and 2 of both sides until the socks measure the appropriate length (see Toe-to-Gusset Length, at right). End your work having just finished side 2, sock A. You are back at your marker and ready to begin the gusset increases.

> ### TOE-TO-GUSSET LENGTH
> Use this handy formula. Note: For Z, measure on side 2 of sock.
>
> **X**   (desired total sock length)   = _____ "
> **Y**   (# of rows in gusset and heel cup) = 45 (S); 53 (L)
> **Z**   (rows per inch)   = _____
> **TGL** (toe-to-gusset length)   = _____ "
>
> $$\underline{\quad\quad}" - (\underline{\quad\quad} \div \underline{\quad\quad}) = \underline{\quad\quad}"$$
> $$\text{X} \qquad\quad \text{Y} \qquad \text{Z} \qquad\quad \text{TGL}$$
>
> For more information, see Toe-Up Math, page 19.

Increasing for the Gussets

Round 1 (increase)
- **SIDE 1 (INSTEP), socks A and B:** Continue to work in stockinette stitch as established.
- **SIDE 2 (SOLE), socks B and A:** K1, M1R, knit to last stitch of each sock, M1L, K1.

Round 2 (even)
- **SIDE 1 (INSTEP), socks A and B:** Continue to work in stockinette stitch as established.
- **SIDE 2 (SOLE), socks B and A:** Work in stockinette stitch as established.

Next Rounds
- Repeat Rounds 1 and 2   **S** 14 more times   **L** 17 more times
- Side 1 (instep) of each sock still has   **S** 30 sts   **L** 36 sts
- Side 2 (sole) of each sock now has   **S** 60 sts   **L** 72 sts

Shaping the Heel Cup, Sock B

Set Up   This is a partial round, worked only on side 1 (instep) of both socks.
- **SIDE 1 (INSTEP), socks A and B:** Work in stockinette stitch as established.
- **ROTATE:** Rotate work and arrange stitches so that you are ready to begin working the heel on side 2 of sock B.

> **NOTE**   While shaping the heel cup and working the heel flap, you temporarily switch to working the socks individually. You first work side 2 of sock B back and forth in short rows, then you work side 2 of sock A in a similar manner. When the heels are completed, you return to knitting the socks together in rounds (in the Knitting the Legs section below). For information about short rows and wrapping stitches, see Tips for Shaping the Heel (page 34).

Side 2, Row 1 (right side)
- Knit   Ⓢ 15 sts   Ⓛ 18 sts
- Place marker 1.
- Knit   Ⓢ 29 sts   Ⓛ 35 sts
- Slip 1 as if to purl, bring yarn to the right side to wrap stitch, place marker 2 on left-hand needle, slip stitch back to left-hand needle. Turn work to the wrong side.

Side 2, Row 2 (wrong side)   Purl to 1 stitch before marker 1, slip 1 as if to purl, bring yarn to right side to wrap stitch, slip stitch back to left-hand needle. Turn work to the right side.

Side 2, Row 3 (right side)   Knit to 2 stitches before previously wrapped stitch, slip 1 as if to purl, bring yarn to right side to wrap stitch, slip stitch back to left-hand needle. Turn.

Side 2, Row 4 (wrong side)   Purl to 2 stitches before previously wrapped stitch, slip 1 as if to purl, bring yarn to right side to wrap stitch, slip stitch back to left-hand needle. Turn.

Next Rows   Repeat Rows 3 and 4 until all but the 4 center stitches have been wrapped. End having just completed   Ⓢ Row 4   Ⓛ Row 3

For Woman's Small Only

Next Row   Knit 3 stitches, slip 1 as if to purl, bring yarn to right side to wrap stitch, slip stitch back to left-hand needle. Turn.

Working the Heel Flap, Sock B

NOTE Continue to work back and forth in rows on side 2, sock B only. During the first two rows of the heel flap, you will be lifting and working the wraps that you created in the heel-cup shaping steps above. For information on lifting and working wraps on the right and wrong side, see Tips for Working Wrapped Stitches (page 38).

Side 2, Row 1 (wrong side) Purl, lifting the wraps and purling them together with their respective stitches as you come to them, to 1 stitch before marker 1. Then, lift the wrap of the stitch before marker 1, slip both stitch and wrap to the right-hand needle as if to purl, remove marker, slip both stitch and wrap back to the left-hand needle, and purl together the wrap and its stitch along with the next stitch (P3tog). Turn.

Side 2, Row 2 (right side) Slip 1 as if to purl. Then knit, lifting the wraps and knitting them together with their respective stitches as you come to them, to 1 stitch before marker 2. Lift the wrap of the next stitch completely over and to the left of the stitch, slip the stitch as if to knit, slip the wrap as if to knit, remove marker, slip next stitch as if to knit, place the 2 slipped stitches and the wrap back on left-hand needle, and knit the 2 slipped stitches together with the wrap through the back loop. Turn.

Side 2, Row 3 (wrong side) Slip 1 as if to purl, purl to 1 stitch before gap, P2tog to close gap. Turn.

Side 2, Row 4 (right side) Slip 1 as if to purl, *K1, slip 1 as if to purl; repeat from * to 1 stitch before gap, ssk to close gap. Turn.

Side 2, Row 5 (wrong side) Slip 1 as if to purl, purl to 1 stitch before gap, P2tog to close gap. Turn.

Next Rows Repeat Rows 4 and 5 until you have decreased away all of the gusset stitches on side 2 of this sock. End having completed a right-side row.
- Side 2 of sock B now again has   **S** 30 sts   **L** 36 sts

Shaping the Heel Cup and Working the Heel Flap, Sock A

To shape the heel cup and work the heel flap of sock A, repeat the instructions for sock B above.

Knitting the Legs

In this section you return to working in the round on all stitches for both socks.

NOTE Pick up an extra stitch at the point where the heel and instep meet to prevent holes from developing. (See Knitting the Legs, pages 41–42.)

Next Round
- SIDE 1 (INSTEP), **socks A and B:** Work across instep stitches according to the Tuscany Chart, beginning at the lower right.
- SIDE 2 (SOLE), **socks B and A:** Work these stitches according to the Tuscany Chart, beginning at the lower right.

Next Rounds Continue working in the round, following the Tuscany Chart on all stitches, until the leg measurement from the top of the heel flap is 5" (13 cm).

Next Rounds Work K1, P1 rib on all stitches for 1½" (3.75 cm).

Finishing

Loosely bind off all stitches using your preferred method (see Bind Offs, pages 159–160). Weave in loose tails. Block.

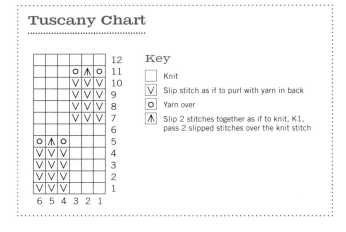

Tuscany Chart

Key

☐ Knit

V Slip stitch as if to purl with yarn in back

O Yarn over

Λ Slip 2 stitches together as if to knit, K1, pass 2 slipped stitches over the knit stitch

On the Town

These delightfully sparkly trouser socks just beg to be knitted. Wear them to work to dress up the day or take them out to dinner. If you would like to make these into knee socks (and you have another skein of yarn), keep knitting until your socks reach to about one inch below your knee. For a touch of playful femininity, weave a one-quarter-inch satin ribbon through the eyelets made by the yarn overs on the final round.

WOMAN'S SIZES	SMALL	LARGE
FINISHED FOOT CIRCUMFERENCE	7½" (19 cm)	9¼" (23.5 cm)
YARN	Kraemer Sterling Silk & Silver, 63% superwash merino/20% silk/15% nylon/2% silver, 3.5 oz (100 g)/420 yds (384 m); Tuxedo: 1 skein	
GAUGE	7 stitches and 10 rows = 1" (2.5 cm) in stockinette stitch	
NEEDLE	US 2 (2.75 mm) 40" (100 cm) circular, *or size needed to obtain correct gauge*	
NOTIONS	3 stitch markers (including 1 locking stitch marker), darning needle	

Pattern Stitches

Stockinette
Knit every round.

Ribbing
*K1,P1; repeat from *.

On the Town (multiple of 6)
See the On the Town Chart on page 73.
Round 1: *K3, yo, slip next 2 stitches together as if to knit, K1, pass 2 slipped stitches over the knit stitch, yo; repeat from *.
Round 2: Knit.
Round 3: *Yo, slip next 2 stitches together as if to knit, K1, pass 2 slipped stitches over the knit stitch, yo, K3; repeat from *.
Round 4: Knit.

Casting On and Shaping the Toes

Cast On Follow the instructions for casting on stitches on pages 23–26 to cast on 16 stitches for sock B and 16 stitches for sock A.

Round 1 Follow the instructions for knitting Round 1 on pages 27–30 to knit the first round on both socks. You now have 8 stitches on side 1 (instep) for each sock and 8 stitches on side 2 (sole) for each sock.

Round 2 (increase)

> **NOTE** All make 1 (M1) increases should be worked with a backward loop increase (see Backward Loop Increases on page 159).

- **SIDE 1 (INSTEP)**, **sock A:** K1, M1R, knit to 1 stitch before the end, M1L, K1.
- **SIDE 1 (INSTEP)**, **sock B:** K1, M1R, knit to 1 stitch before the end, M1L, K1.
- **ROTATE:** Rotate your work and arrange your stitches on the needles so that you are ready to work the sole stitches on side 2 of both socks.
- **SIDE 2 (SOLE)**, **socks B and A:** Repeat the side 1 increases on both socks.
- Each sock now has 20 stitches (10 on each side of each sock).
- **ROTATE:** Rotate your work and arrange stitches so that you are ready to begin the next round.

Next Rounds
- Work Round 2 increases   **S** 3 more times   **L** 4 more times
- Each sock now has   **S** 32 sts   **L** 36 sts

Next Round (even) Knit both sides of socks A and B with no increases.

Next Round (increase) Repeat Round 2.

Next Rounds
- Repeat the last 2 rounds (knit even and increase)
    S 3 more times   **L** 5 more times
- End your work back at the marker having just finished side 2, sock A.
- Each sock now has a total of   **S** 48 sts   **L** 60 sts
- Each side of each sock now has   **S** 24 sts   **L** 30 sts

Knitting the Feet

Round 1

- **SIDE 1** (INSTEP), **socks A and B:** Work the On the Town Chart, beginning at the lower right.
- **SIDE 2** (SOLE), **socks B and A:** Knit to end (stockinette stitch).

Next Rounds Repeat the previous round, continuing to work the On the Town pattern on side 1 of each sock and keeping side 2 in stockinette, until the socks measure the appropriate length (see Toe-to-Gusset Length, above). End your work having just finished side 2, sock A. You are back at your marker and ready to begin the gusset increases.

TOE-TO-GUSSET LENGTH

Use this handy formula. Note: For Z, measure on side 2 of sock.

X (desired total sock length) = _____ "
Y (# of rows in gusset and heel cup) = 35 (S); 45 (L)
Z (rows per inch) = _____
TGL (toe-to-gusset length) = _____ "

$$\frac{\_\_\_\_"}{X} - \left(\frac{\_\_\_\_}{Y} \div \frac{\_\_\_\_}{Z}\right) = \frac{\_\_\_\_"}{TGL}$$

For more information, see Toe-Up Math, page 19.

Increasing for the Gussets

Round 1 (increase)

- **SIDE 1** (INSTEP), **socks A and B:** Continue to work the On the Town Chart as established.
- **SIDE 2** (SOLE), **socks B and A:** K1, M1R, knit to last stitch of each sock, M1L, K1.

Round 2 (even)

- **SIDE 1** (INSTEP), **socks A and B:** Continue to work the On the Town Chart as established.
- **SIDE 2** (SOLE), **socks B and A:** Work in stockinette stitch as established.

Next Rounds

- Repeat Rounds 1 and 2   **S** 11 more times   **L** 14 more times
- Side 1 (instep) of each sock still has   **S** 24 sts   **L** 30 sts
- Side 2 (sole) of each sock now has   **S** 48 sts   **L** 60 sts

Shaping the Heel Cup, Sock B

Set Up This is a partial round, worked only on side 1 (instep) of both socks.
- **SIDE 1 (INSTEP), socks A and B:** Work the On the Town Chart as established.
- **ROTATE:** Rotate work and arrange stitches so that you are ready to begin working the heel on side 2 of sock B.

NOTE While shaping the heel cup and working the heel flap, you temporarily switch to working the socks individually. You first work side 2 of sock B back and forth in short rows, then you work side 2 of sock A in a similar manner. When the heels are completed, you return to knitting the socks together in rounds (in the Knitting the Legs section below). For information about short rows and wrapping stitches, see Tips for Shaping the Heel (page 34).

Side 2, Row 1 (right side)
- Knit   S 12 sts   L 15 sts
- Place marker 1.
- Knit   S 23 sts   L 29 sts
- Slip 1 as if to purl, bring yarn to the right side to wrap stitch, place marker 2 on left-hand needle, slip stitch back to left-hand needle. Turn work to the wrong side.

Side 2, Row 2 (wrong side) Purl to 1 stitch before marker 1, slip 1 as if to purl, bring yarn to right side to wrap stitch, slip stitch back to left-hand needle. Turn work to the right side.

Side 2, Row 3 (right side) Knit to 2 stitches before previously wrapped stitch, slip 1 as if to purl, bring yarn to right side to wrap stitch, slip stitch back to left-hand needle. Turn.

Side 2, Row 4 (wrong side) Purl to 2 stitches before previously wrapped stitch, slip 1 as if to purl, bring yarn to right side to wrap stitch, slip stitch back to left-hand needle. Turn.

Next Rows Repeat Rows 3 and 4 until all but the 4 center stitches have been wrapped. End having just completed   S Row 3   L Row 4

For Woman's Large Only

Next Row Knit 3 stitches, slip 1 as if to purl, bring yarn to right side to wrap stitch, slip stitch back to left-hand needle. Turn.

Working the Heel Flap, Sock B

NOTE Continue to work back and forth in rows on side 2, sock B only. During the first two rows of the heel flap, you will be lifting and working the wraps that you created in the heel-cup shaping steps above. For information on lifting and working wraps on the right and wrong side, see Tips for Working Wrapped Stitches (page 38).

Side 2, Row 1 (wrong side) Purl, lifting the wraps and purling them together with their respective stitches as you come to them, to 1 stitch before marker 1. Then, lift the wrap of the stitch before marker 1, slip both stitch and wrap to the right-hand needle as if to purl, remove marker, slip both stitch and wrap back to the left-hand needle, and purl together the wrap and its stitch along with the next stitch (P3tog). Turn.

Side 2, Row 2 (right side) Slip 1 as if to purl. Then knit, lifting the wraps and knitting them together with their respective stitches as you come to them, to 1 stitch before marker 2. Lift the wrap of the next stitch completely over and to the left of the stitch, slip the stitch as if to knit, slip the wrap as if to knit, remove marker, slip next stitch as if to knit, place the 2 slipped stitches and the wrap back on left-hand needle, and knit the 2 slipped stitches together with the wrap through the back loop. Turn.

Side 2, Row 3 (wrong side) Slip 1 as if to purl, purl to 1 stitch before gap, P2tog to close gap. Turn.

Side 2, Row 4 (right side) Slip 1 as if to purl, *K1, slip 1 as if to purl; repeat from * to 1 stitch before gap, ssk to close gap. Turn.

Side 2, Row 5 (wrong side) Slip 1 as if to purl, purl to 1 stitch before gap, P2tog to close gap. Turn.

Next Rows Repeat Rows 4 and 5 until you have decreased away all of the gusset stitches on side 2 of this sock. End having completed a right-side row.
  • Side 2 of sock B now again has   S 24 sts   L 30 sts

Shaping the Heel Cup and Working the Heel Flap, Sock A

To shape the heel cup and work the heel flap of sock A, repeat the instructions for sock B above.

Knitting the Legs

In this section you return to working in the round on all stitches for both socks.

NOTE Pick up an extra stitch at the point where the heel and instep meet to prevent holes from developing. (See Knitting the Legs, pages 41–42.)

Next Round
- SIDE 1 (INSTEP), **socks A and B:** Work across instep stitches according to the On the Town Chart as established.
- SIDE 2 (SOLE), **socks B and A:** Work these stitches according to the On the Town Chart, following the same row in the chart that you used on side 1.

Next Rounds Continue working in the round, following the On the Town Chart on all stitches, until the leg measurement from the top of the heel flap is

⒮ 8" (20 cm)   ⒧ 9" (23 cm)

Next 8 Rounds Work in K1, P1 rib on all stitches.

Next Round *K1, P1, yo, P2tog. Repeat from * to the end of the round.

Finishing

Loosely bind off all stitches using your preferred method (see Bind Offs, pages 159–160). Weave in loose tails. Block.

On the Town Chart

							4
		○	∧	○			3
							2
○	∧	○					1
6	5	4	3	2	1		

Key

☐ Knit

○ Yarn over

∧ Slip 2 stitches together as if to knit, K1, pass 2 slipped stitches over the knit stitch

Seagrass

I could sit forever and watch the ocean move and shift and change as hours drift by, light changes, and tides move in and out. This gently undulating pattern makes me think of seaweed being pulled gently to and fro by the tide. The colors of Dream in Color yarn never cease to astound me. Not really tonal but not truly variegated either, their subtlety charms and delights me as I knit along. It's soothing to see the colors and the pattern fall away from your needles as you knit.

CHILD'S SIZES	SMALL	LARGE
FINISHED FOOT CIRCUMFERENCE	5¾" (14.5 cm)	7¼" (18.5 cm)
YARN	Dream in Color Smooshy, 100% superfine Australian merino superwash, 4 oz (114 g)/450 yds (411 m) [*Yarn band gauge: 6.5–8 stitches = 1" (2.5 cm) in stockinette stitch on US 1–3 (2.25–3.25 mm) needles*]; Beach Fog: 1 skein	
GAUGE	8 stitches and 11 rows = 1" (2.5 cm) in stockinette stitch	
NEEDLE	US 2 (2.75 mm) 40" (100 cm) circular, *or size needed to obtain correct gauge*	
NOTIONS	3 stitch markers (including 1 locking stitch marker), darning needle	

Pattern Stitches

Seagrass (multiple of 6)
See the Seagrass Chart on page 80.
Rounds 1–2: *K4, P2; repeat from *.
Rounds 3–4: *K3, P3; repeat from *.
Rounds 5–6: *K2, P4; repeat from *.
Rounds 7–8: *K1, P4, K1; repeat from *.
Rounds 9–10: *K1, P3, K2; repeat from *.
Rounds 11–12: *K1, P2, K3; repeat from *.

Ribbing
*K1,P1; repeat from *.

Stockinette
Knit every round.

Casting On and Shaping the Toes

Cast On   Follow the instructions for casting on stitches on pages 23–26 to cast on 12 stitches for sock B and 12 stitches for sock A.

Round 1   Follow the instructions for knitting Round 1 on pages 27–30 to knit the first round on both socks. You now have 6 stitches on side 1 (instep) for each sock and 6 stitches on side 2 (sole) for each sock.

Round 2 (increase)

> NOTE All make 1 (M1) increases should be worked with a backward loop increase (see Backward Loop Increases on page 159).

- **SIDE 1 (INSTEP), sock A:** K1, M1R, knit to 1 stitch before the end, M1L, K1.
- **SIDE 1 (INSTEP), sock B:** K1, M1R, knit to 1 stitch before the end, M1L, K1.
- **ROTATE:** Rotate your work and arrange your stitches on the needles so that you are ready to work the sole stitches on side 2 of both socks.
- **SIDE 2 (SOLE), socks B and A:** Repeat the side 1 increases on both socks.
- Each sock now has 16 stitches (8 on each side of each sock).
- **ROTATE:** Rotate your work and arrange stitches so that you are ready to begin the next round.

Next Rounds
- Work Round 2 increases   S 3 more times   L 5 more times
- Each sock now has   S 28 sts   L 36 sts

Next Round (even)   Knit both sides of socks A and B with no increases.

Next Round (increase)   Repeat Round 2.

Next Rounds
- Repeat the last 2 rounds (knit even and increase)
                                   S 4 more times   L 5 more times
- End your work back at the marker having just finished side 2, sock A.
- Each sock now has a total of   S 48 sts   L 60 sts
- Each side of each sock now has   S 24 sts   L 30 sts

Knitting the Feet

Round 1
- **SIDE 1 (INSTEP), socks A and B:**
  Work the Seagrass Chart, beginning at
  the lower right.
- **SIDE 2 (SOLE), socks B and A:** Knit
  to end (stockinette stitch).

Next Rounds Repeat the previous
round, continuing to work the Seagrass
Chart on side 1 of each sock and keeping
side 2 in stockinette, until the socks measure
the appropriate length (see Toe-to-Gusset Length, above). End your work having just finished side 2, sock A. You are back at your marker and ready to begin the gusset increases.

TOE-TO-GUSSET LENGTH

Use this handy formula. Note: For Z, measure on side 2
of sock.

X (desired total sock length)   = _____ "
Y (# of rows in gusset and heel cup) = 35 (S); 45 (L)
Z (rows per inch)   = _____
TGL (toe-to-gusset length)   = _____ "

$$\underline{\qquad}" - (\underline{\qquad}_X \div \underline{\qquad}_Z) = \underline{\qquad}_{TGL}"$$

For more information, see Toe-Up Math, page 19.

Increasing for the Gussets

Round 1 (increase)
- **SIDE 1 (INSTEP), socks A and B:** Continue to work the Seagrass Chart as
  established.
- **SIDE 2 (SOLE), socks B and A:** K1, M1R, knit to last stitch of each sock, M1L, K1.

Round 2 (even)
- **SIDE 1 (INSTEP), socks A and B:** Continue to work the Seagrass Chart as
  established.
- **SIDE 2 (SOLE), socks B and A:** Work in stockinette stitch as established.

Next Rounds
- Repeat Rounds 1 and 2   **S** 11 more times   **L** 14 more times
- Side 1 (instep) of each sock still has   **S** 24 sts   **L** 30 sts
- Side 2 (sole) of each sock now has   **S** 48 sts   **L** 60 sts

S Small   L Large

Shaping the Heel Cup, Sock B

Set Up   This is a partial round, worked only on side 1 (instep) of both socks.

- **SIDE 1 (INSTEP), socks A and B:** Work the Seagrass Chart as established.
- **ROTATE:** Rotate work and arrange stitches so that you are ready to begin working the heel on side 2 of sock B.

> **NOTE**   While shaping the heel cup and working the heel flap, you temporarily switch to working the socks individually. You first work side 2 of sock B back and forth in short rows, then you work side 2 of sock A in a similar manner. When the heels are completed, you return to knitting the socks together in rounds (in the Knitting the Legs section below). For information about short rows and wrapping stitches, see Tips for Shaping the Heel (page 34).

Side 2, Row 1 (right side)

- Knit   S 12 sts   L 15 sts
- Place marker 1.
- Knit   S 23 sts   L 29 sts
- Slip 1 as if to purl, bring yarn to the right side to wrap stitch, place marker 2 on left-hand needle, slip stitch back to left-hand needle. Turn work to the wrong side.

Side 2, Row 2 (wrong side)   Purl to 1 stitch before marker 1, slip 1 as if to purl, bring yarn to right side to wrap stitch, slip stitch back to left-hand needle. Turn work to the right side.

Side 2, Row 3 (right side)   Knit to 2 stitches before previously wrapped stitch, slip 1 as if to purl, bring yarn to right side to wrap stitch, slip stitch back to left-hand needle. Turn.

Side 2, Row 4 (wrong side)   Purl to 2 stitches before previously wrapped stitch, slip 1 as if to purl, bring yarn to right side to wrap stitch, slip stitch back to left-hand needle. Turn.

Next Rows   Repeat Rows 3 and 4 until all but the 4 center stitches have been wrapped. End having just completed   S Row 3   L Row 4

For Child's Large Only

Next Row   Knit 3 stitches, slip 1 as if to purl, bring yarn to right side to wrap stitch, slip stitch back to left-hand needle. Turn.

Working the Heel Flap, Sock B

NOTE Continue to work back and forth in rows on side 2, sock B only. During the first two rows of the heel flap, you will be lifting and working the wraps that you created in the heel-cup shaping steps above. For information on lifting and working wraps on the right and wrong side, see Tips for Working Wrapped Stitches (page 38).

Side 2, Row 1 (wrong side) Purl, lifting the wraps and purling them together with their respective stitches as you come to them, to 1 stitch before marker 1. Then, lift the wrap of the stitch before marker 1, slip both stitch and wrap to the right-hand needle as if to purl, remove marker, slip both stitch and wrap back to the left-hand needle, and purl together the wrap and its stitch along with the next stitch (P3tog). Turn.

Side 2, Row 2 (right side) Slip 1 as if to purl. Then knit, lifting the wraps and knitting them together with their respective stitches as you come to them, to 1 stitch before marker 2. Lift the wrap of the next stitch completely over and to the left of the stitch, slip the stitch as if to knit, slip the wrap as if to knit, remove marker, slip next stitch as if to knit, place the 2 slipped stitches and the wrap back on left-hand needle, and knit the 2 slipped stitches together with the wrap through the back loop. Turn.

Side 2, Row 3 (wrong side) Slip 1 as if to purl, purl to 1 stitch before gap, P2tog to close gap. Turn.

Side 2, Row 4 (right side) Slip 1 as if to purl, *K1, slip 1 as if to purl; repeat from * to 1 stitch before gap, ssk to close gap. Turn.

Side 2, Row 5 (wrong side) Slip 1 as if to purl, purl to 1 stitch before gap, P2tog to close gap. Turn.

Next Rows Repeat Rows 4 and 5 until you have decreased away all of the gusset stitches on side 2 of this sock. End having completed a right-side row.
  • Side 2 of sock B now again has   S 24 sts   L 30 sts

Shaping the Heel Cup and Working the Heel Flap, Sock A

To shape the heel cup and work the heel flap of sock A, repeat the instructions for sock B above.

Knitting the Legs

In this section you return to working in the round on all stitches for both socks.

> **NOTE** Pick up an extra stitch at the point where the heel and instep meet to prevent holes from developing. (See Knitting the Legs, pages 41–42.)

Next Round
- SIDE 1 (INSTEP), **socks A and B:** Work across instep stitches according to the Seagrass Chart as established.
- SIDE 2 (SOLE), **socks B and A:** Work these stitches according to the Seagrass Chart, following the same row in the chart that you used on side 1.

Next Rounds Continue working in the round, following the Seagrass Chart on all stitches, until the leg measurement from the top of the heel flap is

        ⓢ 3½" (9 cm)   ⓛ 4" (10 cm)

Next Rounds Work K1, P1 rib on all stitches for 1" (2.5 cm).

Finishing

Loosely bind off all stitches using your preferred method (see Bind Offs, pages 159–160). Weave in loose tails. Block.

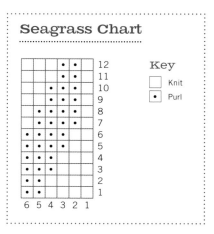

Seagrass Chart

Key

☐ Knit
• Purl

Graphic

One pair of cables traverses the surface of what's really just a simple rib. The cables in this design convey simple strength. This sock is elegant but not a bit pretentious, so it moves comfortably from blue jeans to work pants. The yarn is a soft, washable tweed from Knit Picks, making these fun and affordable to knit.

ADULT'S SIZES	SMALL	LARGE
FINISHED FOOT CIRCUMFERENCE	7¼" (18.5 cm)	8" (20 cm)
YARN	Knit Picks Stroll Tweed, 65% superwash merino wool/25% nylon/10% Donegal, 1.75 oz (50 g)/231 yds (211 m) [*Yarn band gauge: 7–8 stitches = 1" (2.5 cm) in stockinette stitch on US 1–3 (2.25–3.25 mm) needle*]; Plum: 2 skeins for Small; 3 skeins for Large	
GAUGE	8 stitches and 11 rows = 1" (2.5 cm) in stockinette stitch	
NEEDLE	US 2 (2.75 mm) 40" (100 cm) circular, *or size needed to obtain correct gauge*	
NOTIONS	3 stitch markers (including 1 locking stitch marker), cable needle, darning needle	

Pattern Stitches

Stockinette
Knit every round.

Graphic
See the Graphic Charts on pages 88–89.

Ribbing
*K1, P1; repeat from *.

Casting On and Shaping the Toes

Cast On   Follow the instructions for casting on stitches on pages 23–26 to cast on 16 stitches for sock B and 16 stitches for sock A.

Round 1   Follow the instructions for knitting Round 1 on pages 27–30 to knit the first round on both socks. You now have 8 stitches on side 1 (instep) for each sock and 8 stitches on side 2 (sole) for each sock.

Round 2 (increase)

NOTE All make 1 (M1) increases should be worked with a backward loop increase (see Backward Loop Increases on page 159).

- **SIDE 1 (INSTEP), sock A:** K1, M1R, knit to 1 stitch before the end, M1L, K1.
- **SIDE 1 (INSTEP), sock B:** K1, M1R, knit to 1 stitch before the end, M1L, K1.
- **ROTATE:** Rotate your work and arrange your stitches on the needles so that you are ready to work the sole stitches on side 2 of both socks.
- **SIDE 2 (SOLE), socks B and A:** Repeat the side 1 increases on both socks.
- Each sock now has 20 stitches (10 on each side of each sock).
- **ROTATE:** Rotate your work and arrange stitches so that you are ready to begin the next round.

Next Rounds
- Work Round 2 increases   S 5 more times   L 6 more times
- Each sock now has   S 40 sts   L 44 sts

Next Round (even)   Knit both sides of socks A and B with no increases.

Next Round (increase)   Repeat Round 2.

Next Rounds
- Repeat the last 2 rounds (knit even and increase)
                                    S 6 more times   L 7 more times
- End your work back at the marker having just finished side 2, sock A.
- Each sock now has a total of   S 68 sts   L 76 sts
- Each side of each sock now has   S 34 sts   L 38 sts

Knitting the Feet

Round 1

- **SIDE 1 (INSTEP), socks A and B:** Work the Graphic Chart, beginning at the lower right.
- **SIDE 2 (SOLE), socks B and A:** Knit to end (stockinette stitch).

Next Rounds   Repeat the previous round, continuing to work the Graphic Chart on side 1 of each sock and keeping side 2 in stockinette, until the socks measure the appropriate length (see Toe-to-Gusset Length, above). End your work having just finished side 2, sock A. You are back at your marker and ready to begin the gusset increases.

> ### TOE-TO-GUSSET LENGTH
>
> Use this handy formula. Note: For Z, measure on side 2 of sock.
>
> | | | |
> |---|---|---|
> | **X** (desired total sock length) | = _____ " |
> | **Y** (# of rows in gusset and heel cup) | = 51 (S); 57 (L) |
> | **Z** (rows per inch) | = _____ |
> | **TGL** (toe-to-gusset length) | = _____ " |
>
> $$\underset{X}{\_\_\_\_}{}'' - (\underset{Y}{\_\_\_\_} \div \underset{Z}{\_\_\_\_}) = \underset{TGL}{\_\_\_\_}{}''$$
>
> For more information, see Toe-Up Math, page 19.

Increasing for the Gussets

Round 1 (increase)

- **SIDE 1 (INSTEP), socks A and B:** Continue to work the Graphic Chart as established.
- **SIDE 2 (SOLE), socks B and A:** K1, M1R, knit to last stitch of each sock, M1L, K1.

Round 2 (even)

- **SIDE 1 (INSTEP), socks A and B:** Continue to work the Graphic Chart as established.
- **SIDE 2 (SOLE), socks B and A:** Work in stockinette stitch as established.

Next Rounds

- Repeat Rounds 1 and 2   Ⓢ 16 more times   Ⓛ 18 more times
- Side 1 (instep) of each sock still has   Ⓢ 34 sts   Ⓛ 38 sts
- Side 2 (sole) of each sock now has   Ⓢ 68 sts   Ⓛ 76 sts

Shaping the Heel Cup, Sock B

Set Up This is a partial round, worked only on side 1 (instep) of both socks.
- **SIDE 1 (INSTEP), socks A and B:** Work the Graphic Chart as established.
- **ROTATE:** Rotate work and arrange stitches so that you are ready to begin working the heel on side 2 of sock B.

NOTE While shaping the heel cup and working the heel flap, you temporarily switch to working the socks individually. You first work side 2 of sock B back and forth in short rows, then you work side 2 of sock A in a similar manner. When the heels are completed, you return to knitting the socks together in rounds (in the Knitting the Legs section below). For information about short rows and wrapping stitches, see Tips for Shaping the Heel (page 34).

Side 2, Row 1 (right side)
- Knit   ⑤ 17 sts   ⓛ 19 sts
- Place marker 1.
- Knit   ⑤ 33 sts   ⓛ 37 sts
- Slip 1 as if to purl, bring yarn to the right side to wrap stitch, place marker 2 on left-hand needle, slip stitch back to left-hand needle. Turn work to the wrong side.

Side 2, Row 2 (wrong side)
Purl to 1 stitch before marker 1, slip 1 as if to purl, bring yarn to right side to wrap stitch, slip stitch back to left-hand needle. Turn work to the right side.

Side 2, Row 3 (right side)
Knit to 2 stitches before previously wrapped stitch, slip 1 as if to purl, bring yarn to right side to wrap stitch, slip stitch back to left-hand needle. Turn.

Side 2, Row 4 (wrong side)
Purl to 2 stitches before previously wrapped stitch, slip 1 as if to purl, bring yarn to right side to wrap stitch, slip stitch back to left-hand needle. Turn.

Next Rows Repeat Rows 3 and 4 until all but the 4 center stitches have been wrapped. End having just completed Row 4.

Next Row Knit 3 stitches, slip 1 as if to purl, bring yarn to right side to wrap stitch, slip stitch back to left-hand needle. Turn.

Working the Heel Flap, Sock B

NOTE Continue to work back and forth in rows on side 2, sock B only. During the first two rows of the heel flap, you will be lifting and working the wraps that you created in the heel-cup shaping steps above. For information on lifting and working wraps on the right and wrong side, see Tips for Working Wrapped Stitches (page 38).

Side 2, Row 1 (wrong side) Purl, lifting the wraps and purling them together with their respective stitches as you come to them, to 1 stitch before marker 1. Then, lift the wrap of the stitch before marker 1, slip both stitch and wrap to the right-hand needle as if to purl, remove marker, slip both stitch and wrap back to the left-hand needle, and purl together the wrap and its stitch along with the next stitch (P3tog). Turn.

Side 2, Row 2 (right side) Slip 1 as if to purl. Then knit, lifting the wraps and knitting them together with their respective stitches as you come to them, to 1 stitch before marker 2. Lift the wrap of the next stitch completely over and to the left of the stitch, slip the stitch as if to knit, slip the wrap as if to knit, remove marker, slip next stitch as if to knit, place the 2 slipped stitches and the wrap back on left-hand needle, and knit the 2 slipped stitches together with the wrap through the back loop. Turn.

Side 2, Row 3 (wrong side) Slip 1 as if to purl, purl to 1 stitch before gap, P2tog to close gap. Turn.

NOTE From this point on, this heel flap is worked in Eye-of-Partridge Stitch (as written out in Rows 4–7) with a 2-stitch garter-stitch border and 1 edge stitch on each side.

Side 2, Row 4 (right side) Slip 1 as if to purl, K2, *slip 1, K1; repeat from * to 3 stitches before gap, K2, ssk to close gap. Turn.

Side 2, Row 5 (wrong side) Slip 1 as if to purl, K2, purl to 3 stitches before gap, K2, P2tog to close gap. Turn.

Side 2, Row 6 (right side) Slip 1 as if to purl, K2, *K1, slip 1; repeat from * to 3 stitches before gap, K2, ssk to close gap. Turn.

Side 2, Row 7 (wrong side) Slip 1 as if to purl, K2, purl to 3 stitches before gap, K2, P2tog to close gap. Turn.

Next Rows Repeat Rows 4–7 until you have decreased away all of the gusset stitches on side 2 of this sock. End having completed a right-side row.

- Side 2 of sock B now again has   **S** 34 sts   **L** 38 sts

Shaping the Heel Cup and Working the Heel Flap, Sock A

To shape the heel cup and work the heel flap of sock A, repeat the instructions for sock B above.

Knitting the Legs

In this section you return to working in the round on all stitches for both socks.

NOTE Pick up an extra stitch at the point where the heel and instep meet to prevent holes from developing. (See Knitting the Legs, pages 41–42.)

Next Round
- **SIDE 1 (INSTEP), socks A and B:** Work across instep stitches according to the Graphic Chart as established.
- **SIDE 2 (SOLE), socks B and A:** Work these stitches according to the Graphic Chart, following the same row in the chart that you used on side 1.

Next Rounds Continue working in the round, following the Graphic Chart on all stitches until the measurement from the top of the heel flap is approximately

S 5¼" (13.5 cm)   L 5¾" (14.5 cm)

Next Rounds Work K1, P1 rib on all stitches for 2" (5 cm).

Finishing

Loosely bind off all stitches using your preferred method (see Bind Offs, page 159–160). Weave in loose tails. Block.

Graphic Chart for Size Small

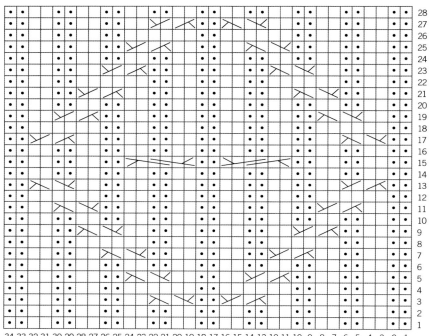

Key

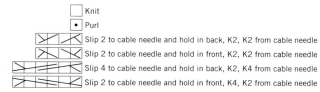

⬜ Knit
• Purl
Slip 2 to cable needle and hold in back, K2, K2 from cable needle
Slip 2 to cable needle and hold in front, K2, K2 from cable needle
Slip 4 to cable needle and hold in back, K2, K4 from cable needle
Slip 2 to cable needle and hold in front, K4, K2 from cable needle

Graphic Chart for Size Large

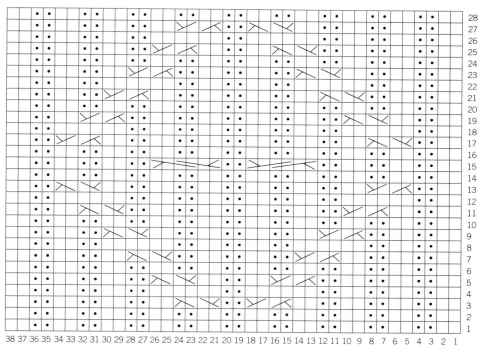

Key

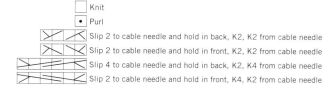

☐ Knit

• Purl

Slip 2 to cable needle and hold in back, K2, K2 from cable needle

Slip 2 to cable needle and hold in front, K2, K2 from cable needle

Slip 4 to cable needle and hold in back, K2, K4 from cable needle

Slip 2 to cable needle and hold in front, K4, K2 from cable needle

April

Once upon a time I was a mom with growing children. Then one day, I became a grandma, and in my first book is a pair of socks for Aidan. But then it happened again, and another little person was placed in my arms. These socks are in honor of my amazing and beautiful granddaughter April, whose big, stormy eyes and enchanting smile have worked their way deeply into my heart. Knitted in a wonderful yarn from Green Mountain Spinnery, these sweet little ankle socks will keep tiny toes warm and toasty.

CHILD'S SIZES	SMALL	LARGE
FINISHED FOOT CIRCUMFERENCE	5" (12.5 cm)	6¾" (17 cm)
YARN	Green Mountain Spinnery Cotton Comfort, 80% fine wool/20% organic cotton, 2 oz (57 g)/180 yds (165 m) [*Yarn band gauge: 5–7½ stitches = 1" (2.5 cm) in stockinette stitch on US 1–6 (2.25–4.0 mm) needles*] • MC = Unbleached White: 1 skein for Small; 2 skeins for Large • CA = Peony: 1 skein • CB = Violet: 1 skein • CC = Yarrow: 1 skein	
GAUGE	6 stitches and 9 rows = 1" (2.5 cm) in stockinette stitch on smaller needle	
NEEDLES	US 3 and US 4 (3.25 mm and 3.5 mm) 40" (100 cm) circulars, *or size needed to obtain correct gauge*	
NOTIONS	3 stitch markers (including 1 locking stitch marker), darning needle	

Pattern Stitches

Stockinette
Knit every round.

Garter
Knit 1 round, purl 1 round.

April
See April Color Chart on page 97.

Reverse Stockinette
Purl every round.

Casting On and Shaping the Toes

Cast On Follow the instructions for casting on stitches on pages 23–26 to cast on 12 stitches for sock B and 12 stitches for sock A.

Round Follow the instructions for knitting Round 1 on pages 27–30 to knit the first round on both socks. You now have 6 stitches on side 1 (instep) for each sock and 6 stitches on side 2 (sole) for each sock.

Round 2 (increase)

NOTE All make 1 (M1) increases should be worked with a backward loop increase (see Backward Loop Increases on page 159).

- **SIDE 1 (INSTEP), sock A:** K1, M1R, knit to 1 stitch before the end, M1L, K1.
- **SIDE 1 (INSTEP), sock B:** K1, M1R, knit to 1 stitch before the end, M1L, K1.
- **ROTATE:** Rotate your work and arrange your stitches on the needles so that you are ready to work the sole stitches on side 2 of both socks.
- **SIDE 2 (SOLE), socks B and A:** Repeat the side 1 increases on both socks.
- Each sock now has 16 stitches (8 on each side of each sock).
- **ROTATE:** Rotate your work and arrange stitches so that you are ready to begin the next round.

Next Rounds

- Work Round 2 increases   **S** 1 more time   **L** 2 more times
- Each sock now has   **S** 20 sts   **L** 24 sts

Next Round (even) Knit both sides of socks A and B with no increases.

Next Round (increase) Repeat Round 2.

Next Rounds

- Repeat the last 2 rounds (knit even and increase)
                              S 2 more times   **L** 3 more times
- End your work back at the marker having just finished side 2, sock A.
- Each sock now has a total of   **S** 32 sts   **L** 40 sts
- Each side of each sock now has **S** 16 sts   **L** 20 sts

Knitting the Feet

Round 1
- **SIDE 1** (INSTEP), **socks A and B:** Work in stockinette stitch.
- **SIDE 2** (SOLE), **socks B and A:** Knit to end (stockinette stitch).

Next Rounds Repeat the previous round, continuing to knit all stitches (stockinette stitch) until the socks measure the appropriate length (see Toe-to-Gusset Length, at right). End your work having just finished side 2, sock A. You are back at your marker and ready to begin the gusset increases.

> ## TOE-TO-GUSSET LENGTH
> Use this handy formula. Note: For Z, measure on side 2 of sock.
>
> **X** (desired total sock length) = _____"
> **Y** (# of rows in gusset and heel cup) = 23 (S); 29 (L)
> **Z** (rows per inch) = _____
> **TGL** (toe-to-gusset length) = _____"
>
> $$\underset{X}{\underline{\quad\quad}}" - (\underset{Y}{\underline{\quad\quad}} \div \underset{Z}{\underline{\quad\quad}}) = \underset{TGL}{\underline{\quad\quad}}"$$
>
> For more information, see Toe-Up Math, page 19.

Increasing for the Gussets

Round 1 (increase)
- **SIDE 1** (INSTEP), **socks A and B:** Continue to work in stockinette stitch as established.
- **SIDE 2** (SOLE), **socks B and A:** K1, M1R, knit to last stitch of each sock, M1L, K1.

Round 2 (even)
- **SIDE 1** (INSTEP), **socks A and B:** Continue to work in stockinette stitch as established.
- **SIDE 2** (SOLE), **socks B and A:** Work in stockinette stitch as established.

Next Rounds
- Repeat Rounds 1 and 2 — **S** 7 more times — **L** 9 more times
- Side 1 (instep) of each sock still has — **S** 16 sts — **L** 20 sts
- Side 2 (sole) of each sock now has — **S** 32 sts — **L** 40 sts

Ⓢ Small   Ⓛ Large

Shaping the Heel Cup, Sock B

Set Up This is a partial round, worked only on side 1 (instep) of both socks.
- **SIDE 1** (INSTEP), **socks A and B:** Work in stockinette stitch as established.
- **ROTATE:** Rotate work and arrange stitches so that you are ready to begin working the heel on side 2 of sock B.

> **NOTE** While shaping the heel cup and working the heel flap, you temporarily switch to working the socks individually. You first work side 2 of sock B back and forth in short rows, then you work side 2 of sock A in a similar manner. When the heels are completed, you return to knitting the socks together in rounds (in the Knitting the Legs section below). For information about short rows and wrapping stitches, see Tips for Shaping the Heel (page 34).

Side 2, Row 1 (right side)
- Knit   Ⓢ 8 sts   Ⓛ 10 sts
- Place marker 1.
- Knit   Ⓢ 15 sts   Ⓛ 19 sts
- Slip 1 as if to purl, bring yarn to the right side to wrap stitch, place marker 2 on left-hand needle, slip stitch back to left-hand needle. Turn work to the wrong side.

Side 2, Row 2 (wrong side) Purl to 1 stitch before marker 1, slip 1 as if to purl, bring yarn to right side to wrap stitch, slip stitch back to left-hand needle. Turn work to the right side.

Side 2, Row 3 (right side) Knit to 2 stitches before previously wrapped stitch, slip 1 as if to purl, bring yarn to right side to wrap stitch, slip stitch back to left-hand needle. Turn.

Side 2, Row 4 (wrong side) Purl to 2 stitches before previously wrapped stitch, slip 1 as if to purl, bring yarn to right side to wrap stitch, slip stitch back to left-hand needle. Turn.

Next Rows Repeat Rows 3 and 4 until all but the 4 center stitches have been wrapped. End having just completed Row 3.

Working the Heel Flap, Sock B

NOTE Continue to work back and forth in rows on side 2, sock B only. During the first two rows of the heel flap, you will be lifting and working the wraps that you created in the heel-cup shaping steps above. For information on lifting and working wraps on the right and wrong side, see Tips for Working Wrapped Stitches (page 38).

Side 2, Row 1 (wrong side) Purl, lifting the wraps and purling them together with their respective stitches as you come to them, to 1 stitch before marker 1. Then, lift the wrap of the stitch before marker 1, slip both stitch and wrap to the right-hand needle as if to purl, remove marker, slip both stitch and wrap back to the left-hand needle, and purl together the wrap and its stitch along with the next stitch (P3tog). Turn.

Side 2, Row 2 (right side) Slip 1 as if to purl. Then knit, lifting the wraps and knitting them together with their respective stitches as you come to them, to 1 stitch before marker 2. Lift the wrap of the next stitch completely over and to the left of the stitch, slip the stitch as if to knit, slip the wrap as if to knit, remove marker, slip next stitch as if to knit, place the 2 slipped stitches and the wrap back on left-hand needle, and knit the 2 slipped stitches together with the wrap through the back loop. Turn.

Side 2, Row 3 (wrong side) Slip 1 as if to purl, purl to 1 stitch before gap, P2tog to close gap. Turn.

Side 2, Row 4 (right side) Slip 1 as if to purl, *K1, slip 1 as if to purl; repeat from * to 1 stitch before gap, ssk to close gap. Turn.

Side 2, Row 5 (wrong side) Slip 1 as if to purl, purl to 1 stitch before gap, P2tog to close gap. Turn.

Next Rows Repeat Rows 4 and 5 until you have decreased away all of the gusset stitches on side 2 of this sock. End having completed a right-side row.
• Side 2 of sock B now again has   S 16 sts   L 20 sts

Shaping the Heel Cup and Working the Heel Flap, Sock A

To shape the heel cup and work the heel flap of sock A, repeat the instructions for sock B above.

Knitting the Legs

In this section you return to working in the round on all stitches for both socks.

> **NOTE** Pick up an extra stitch at the point where the heel and instep meet to prevent holes from developing. (See Knitting the Legs, page 41–42.)

Next Round
- SIDE 1 (INSTEP), **socks A and B:** Work across instep stitches in stockinette stitch as established.
- SIDE 2 (SOLE), **socks B and A:** Work these stitches in stockinette stitch.

Next Rounds Continue working in the round in stockinette stitch on all stitches until the leg measurement from the top of the heel flap is

⑤ 2" (5 cm)   ⓛ 2½" (6.4 cm)

Next 4 Rounds Work all stitches in garter stitch beginning with a purl round.

> **NOTE** From this point on, the side facing you as you knit is the wrong side of the turned cuff. The April Color Chart is worked in reverse stockinette (purl stitches) so that it appears as stockinette when the cuff is turned down. As you are working the chart, be sure to "strand" the yarn across the side facing you (the wrong side of the cuff). For more information on knitting with more than one color, see Stranding, page 161.

Next 11 Rounds Change to larger needle. Work the April Color Chart in reverse stockinette stitch.

Next 4 Rounds Change to smaller needle and work all stitches in garter stitch beginning with a knit round.

Finishing

Loosely bind off all stitches using your preferred method (see Bind Offs, pages 159–160). Weave in loose tails. Block. Turn cuff to the right side.

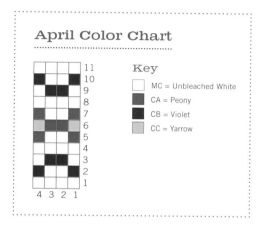

April Color Chart

Key

MC = Unbleached White
CA = Peony
CB = Violet
CC = Yarrow

Ballet

This was the first sock I designed for this book — in fact, I designed it long before I began work on the book. I woke up one morning at about 2 A.M. with a sock in my mind. (I keep a notebook beside my bed for just such occasions!) I made a quick sketch, and then, first thing in the morning, I swatched for this sock. Worked in a simple, light-colored yarn, the twisted stitches weave gracefully in and out, reminiscent of a delicate dance.

WOMAN'S SIZES	SMALL	LARGE
FINISHED FOOT CIRCUMFERENCE	7" (18 cm)	8½" (21.5 cm)
YARN	Valley Yarns Huntington, 75% merino wool/25% nylon, 1.75 oz (50 g)/218 yds (199 m) [*Yarn band gauge: 7–8 stitches = 1" (2.5 cm) on US 2–3 (2.75–3.25 mm) needles*]; Pink 4192: 2 skeins for Small; 3 skeins for Large	
GAUGE	9 stitches and 11 rows = 1" (2.5 cm) in stockinette stitch	
NEEDLE	US 1 (2.25 mm) 40" (100 cm) circular, *or size needed to obtain correct gauge*	
NOTIONS	3 stitch markers (including 1 locking stitch marker), cable needle, darning needle	

Pattern Stitches

Stockinette
Knit every round.

Ballet
See the Ballet Charts on pages 104–105.

Ballet Rib
See the Ballet Rib Charts on page 105.

Casting On and Shaping the Toes

Cast On   Follow the instructions for casting on stitches on pages 23–26 to cast on 16 stitches for sock B and 16 stitches for sock A.

Round 1   Follow the instructions for knitting Round 1 on pages 27–30 to knit the first round on both socks. You now have 8 stitches on side 1 (instep) for each sock and 8 stitches on side 2 (sole) for each sock.

Round 2 (increase)

NOTE All make 1 (M1) increases should be worked with a backward loop increase (see Backward Loop Increases on page 159).

- **SIDE 1 (INSTEP), sock A:** K1, M1R, knit to 1 stitch before the end, M1L, K1.
- **SIDE 1 (INSTEP), sock B:** K1, M1R, knit to 1 stitch before the end, M1L, K1.
- **ROTATE:** Rotate your work and arrange your stitches on the needles so that you are ready to work the sole stitches on side 2 of both socks.
- **SIDE 2 (SOLE), socks B and A:** Repeat the side 1 increases on both socks.
- Each sock now has 20 stitches (10 on each side of each sock).
- **ROTATE:** Rotate your work and arrange stitches so that you are ready to begin the next round.

Next Rounds
- Work Round 2 increases   **S** 6 more times   **L** 8 more times
- Each sock now has   **S** 44 sts   **L** 52 sts

Next Round (even)   Knit both sides of socks A and B with no increases.

Next Round (increase)   Repeat Round 2.

Next Rounds
- Repeat the last 2 rounds (knit even and increase)
  S 6 more times   **L** 8 more times
- End your work back at the marker having just finished side 2, sock A.
- Each sock now has a total of   **S** 72 sts   **L** 88 sts
- Each side of each sock now has **S** 36 sts   **L** 44 sts

Knitting the Feet

Round 1
- **SIDE 1 (INSTEP), socks A and B:** Work the Ballet Chart, beginning at the lower right.
- **SIDE 2 (SOLE), socks B and A:** Knit to end (stockinette stitch).

Next Rounds Repeat the previous round, continuing to work the Ballet Chart on side 1 of each sock and keeping side 2 in stockinette, until the socks measure the appropriate length (see Toe-to-Gusset Length, above). End your work having just finished side 2, sock A. You are back at your marker and ready to begin the gusset increases.

TOE-TO-GUSSET LENGTH

Use this handy formula. Note: For Z, measure on side 2 of sock.

X (desired total sock length)	= _____ "
Y (# of rows in gusset and heel cup)	= 53 (S); 65 (L)
Z (rows per inch)	= _____
TGL (toe-to-gusset length)	= _____ "

$$\underline{\quad\quad}" - (\underline{\quad\quad} \div \underline{\quad\quad}) = \underline{\quad\quad}"$$
$$X \qquad\qquad Y \qquad Z \qquad\qquad TGL$$

For more information, see Toe-Up Math, page 19.

Increasing for the Gussets

Round 1 (increase)
- **SIDE 1 (INSTEP), socks A and B:** Continue to work the Ballet Chart as established.
- **SIDE 2 (SOLE), socks B and A:** K1, M1R, knit to last stitch of each sock, M1L, K1.

Round 2 (even)
- **SIDE 1 (INSTEP), socks A and B:** Continue to work the Ballet Chart as established.
- **SIDE 2 (SOLE), socks B and A:** Work in stockinette stitch as established.

Next Rounds
- Repeat Rounds 1 and 2   Ⓢ 17 more times   Ⓛ 21 more times
- Side 1 (instep) of each sock still has   Ⓢ 36 sts   Ⓛ 44 sts
- Side 2 (sole) of each sock now has   Ⓢ 72 sts   Ⓛ 88 sts

Shaping the Heel Cup, Sock B

Set Up This is a partial round, worked only on side 1 (instep) of both socks.
- **SIDE 1 (INSTEP), socks A and B:** Work the Ballet Chart as established.
- **ROTATE:** Rotate work and arrange stitches so that you are ready to begin working the heel on side 2 of sock B.

NOTE While shaping the heel cup and working the heel flap, you temporarily switch to working the socks individually. You first work side 2 of sock B back and forth in short rows, then you work side 2 of sock A in a similar manner. When the heels are completed, you return to knitting the socks together in rounds (in the Knitting the Legs section below). For information about short rows and wrapping stitches, see Tips for Shaping the Heel (page 34).

Side 2, Row 1 (right side)
- Knit   Ⓢ 18 sts   Ⓛ 22 sts
- Place marker 1.
- Knit   Ⓢ 35 sts   Ⓛ 43 sts
- Slip 1 as if to purl, bring yarn to the right side to wrap stitch, place marker 2 on left-hand needle, slip stitch back to left-hand needle. Turn work to the wrong side.

Side 2, Row 2 (wrong side) Purl to 1 stitch before marker 1, slip 1 as if to purl, bring yarn to right side to wrap stitch, slip stitch back to left-hand needle. Turn work to the right side.

Side 2, Row 3 (right side) Knit to 2 stitches before previously wrapped stitch, slip 1 as if to purl, bring yarn to right side to wrap stitch, slip stitch back to left-hand needle. Turn.

Side 2, Row 4 (wrong side) Purl to 2 stitches before previously wrapped stitch, slip 1 as if to purl, bring yarn to right side to wrap stitch, slip stitch back to left-hand needle. Turn.

Next Rows Repeat Rows 3 and 4 until all but the 4 center stitches have been wrapped. End having just completed Row 3.

Working the Heel Flap, Sock B

NOTE Continue to work back and forth in rows on side 2, sock B only. During the first two rows of the heel flap, you will be lifting and working the wraps that you created in the heel-cup shaping steps above. For information on lifting and working wraps on the right and wrong side, see Tips for Working Wrapped Stitches (page 38).

Side 2, Row 1 (wrong side) Purl, lifting the wraps and purling them together with their respective stitches as you come to them, to 1 stitch before marker 1. Then, lift the wrap of the stitch before marker 1, slip both stitch and wrap to the right-hand needle as if to purl, remove marker, slip both stitch and wrap back to the left-hand needle, and purl together the wrap and its stitch along with the next stitch (P3tog). Turn.

Side 2, Row 2 (right side) Slip 1 as if to purl. Then knit, lifting the wraps and knitting them together with their respective stitches as you come to them, to 1 stitch before marker 2. Lift the wrap of the next stitch completely over and to the left of the stitch, slip the stitch as if to knit, slip the wrap as if to knit, remove marker, slip next stitch as if to knit, place the 2 slipped stitches and the wrap back on left-hand needle, and knit the 2 slipped stitches together with the wrap through the back loop. Turn.

Side 2, Row 3 (wrong side) Slip 1 as if to purl, purl to 1 stitch before gap, P2tog to close gap. Turn.

Side 2, Row 4 (right side) Slip 1 as if to purl, *K1, slip 1 as if to purl; repeat from * to 1 stitch before gap, ssk to close gap. Turn.

Side 2, Row 5 (wrong side) Slip 1 as if to purl, purl to 1 stitch before gap, P2tog to close gap. Turn.

Next Rows Repeat Rows 4 and 5 until you have decreased away all of the gusset stitches on side 2 of this sock. End having completed a right-side row.
   • Side 2 of sock B now again has   S 36 sts   L 44 sts

Shaping the Heel Cup and Working the Heel Flap, Sock A

To shape the heel cup and work the heel flap of sock A, repeat the instructions for sock B above.

Knitting the Legs

In this section you return to working in the round on all stitches for both socks.

NOTE Pick up an extra stitch at the point where the heel and instep meet to prevent holes from developing. (See Knitting the Legs, page 41–42.)

Next Round
   • **SIDE 1 (INSTEP), socks A and B:** Work across instep stitches according to the Ballet Chart as established.
   • **SIDE 2 (SOLE), socks B and A:** Work these stitches according to the Ballet Chart, following the same row in the chart that you used on side 1.

Next Rounds Continue working in the round, following the Ballet Chart for all stitches, until the leg measurement from the top of the heel flap is approximately 5" (12.5 cm). The stitch pattern will line up more closely with the ribbing if you end on Row 4 or Row 20 of the Ballet Chart.

Next Rounds Work the Ballet Rib Chart on all stitches, beginning at the right, until the ribbing measures 1" (2.5 cm).

Finishing

Loosely bind off all stitches using your preferred method (see Bind Offs, pages 159–160). Weave in loose tails. Block.

Ballet Chart for Size Small

Rows (right side, bottom to top): 1, 2, 3, 4, 5, 6, 7, 8, 9, 10, 11, 12, 13, 14, 15, 16, 17, 18, 19, 20

Columns (right to left): 36 35 34 33 32 31 30 29 28 27 26 25 24 23 22 21 20 19 18 17 16 15 14 13 12 11 10 9 8 7 6 5 4 3 2 1

Key

☐	Knit
•	Purl
⟋⟍	Right Twist. Slip 1 to cable needle and hold in back, K1, K1 from cable needle
⟍⟋	Left Twist. Slip 1 to cable needle and hold in front, K1, K1 from cable needle
⟍⟍	Left Twist, purl beginning. Slip 1 to cable needle and hold in front, P1, K1 from cable needle
⟋⟋	Right Twist, purl beginning. Slip 1 to cable needle and hold in back, K1, P1 from cable needle

Ballet Rib Chart for Size Small

36 35 34 33 32 31 30 29 28 27 26 25 24 23 22 21 20 19 18 17 16 15 14 13 12 11 10 9 8 7 6 5 4 3 2 1

1

Key

Knit

• Purl

Ballet Chart for Size Large

20
19
18
17
16
15
14
13
12
11
10
9
8
7
6
5
4
3
2
1

44 43 42 41 40 39 38 37 36 35 34 33 32 31 30 29 28 27 26 25 24 23 22 21 20 19 18 17 16 15 14 13 12 11 10 9 8 7 6 5 4 3 2 1

Key

Knit

• Purl

Right Twist. Slip 1 to cable needle and hold in back, K1, K1 from cable needle

Left Twist. Slip 1 to cable needle and hold in front, K1, K1 from cable needle

Left Twist, purl beginning. Slip 1 to cable needle and hold in front, P1, K1 from cable needle

Right Twist, purl beginning. Slip 1 to cable needle and hold in back, K1, P1 from cable needle

Ballet Rib Chart for Size Large

44 43 42 41 40 39 38 37 36 35 34 33 32 31 30 29 28 27 26 25 24 23 22 21 20 19 18 17 16 15 14 13 12 11 10 9 8 7 6 5 4 3 2 1

1

Key

Knit

• Purl

Twisted Baskets

Take a basic basket-weave pattern, and jazz it up a bit with some simple cable twists. Knitted in medium-weight Socks That Rock, these socks knit up in no time and promise luxurious warmth for the most finicky of feet. This is a great pattern choice for a new sock knitter looking for something a little fun.

ADULT'S SIZES	SMALL	LARGE
FINISHED FOOT CIRCUMFERENCE	7½" (19 cm)	8½" (21.5 cm)
YARN	Blue Moon Fiber Arts Socks That Rock Mediumweight, 100% superwash merino, 5.5 oz (155 g)/380 yds (347 m) [*Yarn band gauge: 7–8 stitches = 1" (2.5 cm) in stockinette stitch on US 2–3 (2.75–3.25 mm) needles*]; Mossay: 1 skein	
GAUGE	7 stitches and 9 rows = 1" (2.5 cm) in stockinette stitch	
NEEDLE	US 3 (3.25.mm) 40" (100 cm) circular, *or size needed to obtain correct gauge*	
NOTIONS	3 stitch markers (including 1 locking stitch marker), cable needle, darning needle	

Pattern Stitches

Twisted Baskets (multiple of 8)
See the Twisted Baskets Chart on page 112.

Stockinette
Knit every round.

Ribbing
*K1, P1; repeat from *.

Casting On and Shaping the Toes

Cast On   Follow the instructions for casting on stitches on pages 23–26 to cast on 16 stitches for sock B and 16 stitches for sock A.

Round 1   Follow the instructions for knitting Round 1 on pages 27–30 to knit the first round on both socks. You now have 8 stitches on side 1 (instep) for each sock and 8 stitches on side 2 (sole) for each sock.

Round 2 (increase)

NOTE All make 1 (M1) increases should be worked with a backward loop increase (see Backward Loop Increases on page 159).

- **SIDE 1** (INSTEP), **sock A:** K1, M1R, knit to 1 stitch before the end, M1L, K1.
- **SIDE 1** (INSTEP), **sock B:** K1, M1R, knit to 1 stitch before the end, M1L, K1.
- **ROTATE:** Rotate your work and arrange your stitches on the needles so that you are ready to work the sole stitches on side 2 of both socks.
- **SIDE 2** (SOLE), **socks B and A:** Repeat the side 1 increases on both socks.
- Each sock now has 20 stitches (10 on each side of each sock).
- **ROTATE:** Rotate your work and arrange stitches so that you are ready to begin the next round.

Next Rounds
- Work Round 2 increases   Ⓢ 4 more times   Ⓛ 5 more times
- Each sock now has   Ⓢ 36 sts   Ⓛ 40 sts

Next Round (even)   Knit both sides of socks A and B with no increases.

Next Round (increase)   Repeat Round 2.

Next Rounds
- Repeat the last 2 rounds (knit even and increase)
                                             Ⓢ 4 more times   Ⓛ 5 more times
- End your work back at the marker having just finished side 2, sock A.
- Each sock now has a total of   Ⓢ 56 sts   Ⓛ 64 sts
- Each side of each sock now has   Ⓢ 28 sts   Ⓛ 32 sts

Knitting the Feet

Round 1

- **SIDE 1** (INSTEP), **socks A and B:** Work the Twisted Baskets Chart, beginning at the lower right. If you are knitting the small size, work three-and-a-half repeats of the stitch pattern across side 1 of each sock; if you are knitting the large size, work four full repeats.
- **SIDE 2** (SOLE), **socks B and A:** Knit to end (stockinette stitch).

> ## TOE-TO-GUSSET LENGTH
> Use this handy formula. Note: For Z, measure on side 2 of sock.
>
> **X** (desired total sock length)   = _____ "
> **Y** (# of rows in gusset and heel cup) = 41 (S); 47 (L)
> **Z** (rows per inch)   = _____
> **TGL** (toe-to-gusset length)   = _____ "
>
> $$\underline{\hspace{2cm}}" - (\underline{\hspace{1.5cm}} \div \underline{\hspace{1.5cm}}) = \underline{\hspace{1.5cm}}"$$
> $$\quad\text{X}\qquad\qquad\text{Y}\qquad\text{Z}\qquad\qquad\text{TGL}$$
>
> For more information, see Toe-Up Math, page 19.

Next Rounds Repeat the previous round, continuing to work the Twisted Baskets Chart on side 1 of each sock and keeping side 2 in stockinette, until the socks measure the appropriate length (see Toe-to-Gusset Length, above). End your work having just finished side 2, sock A. You are back at your marker and ready to begin the gusset increases.

Increasing for the Gussets

Round 1 (increase)

- **SIDE 1** (INSTEP), **socks A and B:** Continue to work the Twisted Baskets Chart as established.
- **SIDE 2** (SOLE), **socks B and A:** K1, M1R, knit to last stitch of each sock, M1L, K1.

Round 2 (even)

- **SIDE 1** (INSTEP), **socks A and B:** Continue to work Twisted Baskets Chart as established.
- **SIDE 2** (SOLE), **socks B and A:** Work in stockinette stitch as established.

Next Rounds

- Repeat Rounds 1 and 2   **S** 13 more times   **L** 15 more times
- Side 1 (instep) of each sock still has   **S** 28 sts   **L** 32 sts
- Side 2 (sole) of each sock now has   **S** 56 sts   **L** 64 sts

Shaping the Heel Cup, Sock B

Set Up This is a partial round, worked only on side 1 (instep) of both socks.
- **SIDE 1** (INSTEP), **socks A and B:** Work the Twisted Baskets Chart as established.
- **ROTATE:** Rotate work and arrange stitches so that you are ready to begin working the heel on side 2 of sock B.

> **NOTE** While shaping the heel cup and working the heel flap, you temporarily switch to working the socks individually. You first work side 2 of sock B back and forth in short rows, then you work side 2 of sock A in a similar manner. When the heels are completed, you return to knitting the socks together in rounds (in the Knitting the Legs section below). For information about short rows and wrapping stitches, see Tips for Shaping the Heel (page 34).

Side 2, Row 1 (right side)
- Knit   S 14 sts   L 16 sts
- Place marker 1.
- Knit   S 27 sts   L 31 sts
- Slip 1 as if to purl, bring yarn to the right side to wrap stitch, place marker 2 on left-hand needle, slip stitch back to left-hand needle. Turn work to the wrong side.

Side 2, Row 2 (wrong side) Purl to 1 stitch before marker 1, slip 1 as if to purl, bring yarn to right side to wrap stitch, slip stitch back to left-hand needle. Turn work to the right side.

Side 2, Row 3 (right side) Knit to 2 stitches before previously wrapped stitch, slip 1 as if to purl, bring yarn to right side to wrap stitch, slip stitch back to left-hand needle. Turn.

Side 2, Row 4 (wrong side) Purl to 2 stitches before previously wrapped stitch, slip 1 as if to purl, bring yarn to right side to wrap stitch, slip stitch back to left-hand needle. Turn.

Next Rows Repeat Rows 3 and 4 until all but the 4 center stitches have been wrapped. End having just completed Row 3.

Working the Heel Flap, Sock B

NOTE Continue to work back and forth in rows on side 2, sock B only. During the first two rows of the heel flap, you will be lifting and working the wraps that you created in the heel-cup shaping steps above. For information on lifting and working wraps on the right and wrong side, see Tips for Working Wrapped Stitches (page 38).

Side 2, Row 1 (wrong side) Purl, lifting the wraps and purling them together with their respective stitches as you come to them, to 1 stitch before marker 1. Then, lift the wrap of the stitch before marker 1, slip both stitch and wrap to the right-hand needle as if to purl, remove marker, slip both stitch and wrap back to the left-hand needle, and purl together the wrap and its stitch along with the next stitch (P3tog). Turn.

Side 2, Row 2 (right side) Slip 1 as if to purl. Then knit, lifting the wraps and knitting them together with their respective stitches as you come to them, to 1 stitch before marker 2. Lift the wrap of the next stitch completely over and to the left of the stitch, slip the stitch as if to knit, slip the wrap as if to knit, remove marker, slip next stitch as if to knit, place the 2 slipped stitches and the wrap back on left-hand needle, and knit the 2 slipped stitches together with the wrap through the back loop. Turn.

Side 2, Row 3 (wrong side) Slip 1 as if to purl, purl to 1 stitch before gap, P2tog to close gap. Turn.

NOTE From this point on, this heel flap is worked in Eye-of-Partridge Stitch (as written out in Rows 4–7) with a 2-stitch garter-stitch border and 1 edge stitch on each side.

Side 2, Row 4 (right side) Slip 1 as if to purl, K2, *slip 1, K1; repeat from * to 3 stitches before gap, K2, ssk to close gap. Turn.

Side 2, Row 5 (wrong side) Slip 1 as if to purl, K2, purl to 3 stitches before gap, K2, P2tog to close gap. Turn.

Side 2, Row 6 (right side) Slip 1 as if to purl, K2, *K1, slip 1; repeat from * to 3 stitches before gap, K2, ssk to close gap. Turn.

Side 2, Row 7 (wrong side) Slip 1 as if to purl, K2, purl to 3 stitches before gap, K2, P2tog to close gap. Turn.

Next Rows Repeat Rows 4–7 until you have decreased away all of the gusset stitches on side 2 of this sock. End having completed a right-side row.

- Side 2 of sock B now again has   **S** 28 sts   **L** 32 sts

Shaping the Heel Cup and Working the Heel Flap, Sock A

To shape the heel cup and work the heel flap of sock A, repeat the instructions for sock B above.

Knitting the Legs

In this section you return to working in the round on all stitches for both socks.

NOTE Pick up an extra stitch at the point where the heel and instep meet to prevent holes from developing. (See Knitting the Legs, pages 41–42.)

Next Round
- **SIDE 1 (INSTEP), socks A and B:** Work across instep stitches according to the Twisted Baskets Chart as established.
- **SIDE 2 (SOLE), socks B and A:** Work these stitches according to the Twisted Baskets Chart, following the same row in the chart that you used on side 1. If you are knitting the small size, there will be only three-and-a-half repeats of the stitch pattern on each side of each sock. When working side 2, make sure you begin with the column of the chart that you left off with on side 1 (column 5).

Next Rounds Continue working in the round, following the Twisted Baskets Chart for all stitches, until the leg measurement from the top of the heel flap is

S 4" (10 cm)   L 4½" (11.5 cm)

Next Rounds Work K1, P1 rib on all stitches for 1½" (3.75 cm).

Finishing

Loosely bind off all stitches using your preferred method (see Bind Offs, pages 159–160). Weave in loose tails. Block.

Twisted Baskets Chart

Key

☐	Knit
•	Purl
⟩⟨	Slip 2 stitches to cable needle and hold in front, K1, K2 from cable needle

Simplicity

It would probably be appropriate to call this a "guy sock" if only because most guys seem to prefer understated socks with very little flash. In this simple workhorse sock there's enough going on in the ribbed pattern to keep the knitter from getting bored, which is always a good thing, while the pattern itself remains simple enough for even the most selective of wearers. That's the nice way to say that this is a great simple sock for fussy folk!

ADULT'S SIZES	SMALL	LARGE
FINISHED FOOT CIRCUMFERENCE	7" (18 cm)	8½" (21.5 cm)
YARN	Schaefer Yarn Heather, 55% merino wool superwash/30% cultivated silk/15% nylon, 4 oz (114 g)/400 yds (366 m) [*Yarn band gauge: 7–8 stitches = 1" (2.5 cm) in stockinette stitch on US 1 (2.25.mm) needles*]; Elizabeth Blackwell: 1 skein	
GAUGE	8 stitches and 10 rows = 1" (2.5 cm) in stockinette stitch	
NEEDLE	US 1 (2.25 mm) 40" (100 cm) circular, *or size needed to obtain correct gauge*	
NOTIONS	3 stitch markers (including 1 locking stitch marker), darning needle	

Pattern Stitches

Ribbing
*K1, P1; repeat from *.

Stockinette
Knit every round.

Simplicity
See the Simplicity Charts on page 119.

Casting On and Shaping the Toes

Cast On Follow the instructions for casting on stitches on pages 23–26 to cast on 16 stitches for sock B and 16 stitches for sock A.

Round 1 Follow the instructions for knitting Round 1 on pages 27–30 to knit the first round on both socks. You now have 8 stitches on side 1 (instep) for each sock and 8 stitches on side 2 (sole) for each sock.

Round 2 (increase)

NOTE All make 1 (M1) increases should be worked with a backward loop increase (see Backward Loop Increases on page 159.)

- **SIDE 1 (INSTEP), sock A:** K1, M1R, knit to 1 stitch before the end, M1L, K1.
- **SIDE 1 (INSTEP), sock B:** K1, M1R, knit to 1 stitch before the end, M1L, K1.
- **ROTATE:** Rotate your work and arrange your stitches on the needles so that you are ready to work the sole stitches on side 2 of both socks.
- **SIDE 2 (SOLE), socks B and A:** Repeat the side 1 increases on both socks.
- Each sock now has 20 stitches (10 on each side of each sock).
- **ROTATE:** Rotate your work and arrange stitches so that you are ready to begin the next round.

Next Rounds
- Work Round 2 increases   S 5 more times   L 6 more times
- Each sock now has   S 40 sts   L 44 sts

Next Round (even) Knit both sides of socks A and B with no increases.

Next Round (increase) Repeat Round 2.

Next Rounds
- Repeat the last 2 rounds (knit even and increase)
                                      S 4 more times   L 6 more times
- End your work back at the marker having just finished side 2, sock A.
- Each sock now has a total of   S 60 sts   L 72 sts
- Each side of each sock now has   S 30 sts   L 36 sts

Knitting the Feet

Round 1
- **SIDE 1** (INSTEP), **socks A and B:** Work the Simplicity Chart, beginning at the lower right.
- **SIDE 2** (SOLE), **socks B and A:** Knit to end (stockinette stitch).

Next Rounds Repeat the previous round, continuing to work the Simplicity Chart on side 1 of each sock and keeping side 2 in stockinette, until the socks measure the appropriate length (see Toe-to-Gusset Length, above). End your work having just finished side 2, sock A. You are back at your marker and ready to begin the gusset increases.

TOE-TO-GUSSET LENGTH

Use this handy formula. Note: For Z, measure on side 2 of sock.

X (desired total sock length)	= _____ "
Y (# of rows in gusset and heel cup)	= 45 (S); 53 (L)
Z (rows per inch)	= _____
TGL (toe-to-gusset length)	= _____ "

$$\underbrace{\text{_____}}_{X}{}'' - (\underbrace{\text{_____}}_{Y} \div \underbrace{\text{_____}}_{Z}) = \underbrace{\text{_____}}_{TGL}{}''$$

For more information, see Toe-Up Math, page 19.

Increasing for the Gussets

Round 1 (increase)
- **SIDE 1** (INSTEP), **socks A and B:** Continue to work the Simplicity Chart as established.
- **SIDE 2** (SOLE), **socks B and A:** K1, M1R, knit to last stitch of each sock, M1L, K1.

Round 2 (even)
- **SIDE 1** (INSTEP), **socks A and B:** Continue to work the Simplicity Chart as established.
- **SIDE 2** (SOLE), **socks B and A:** Work in stockinette stitch as established.

Next Rounds
- Repeat Rounds 1 and 2
- Side 1 (instep) of each sock still has
- Side 2 (sole) of each sock now has

	Ⓢ	Ⓛ
Repeat Rounds 1 and 2	14 more times	17 more times
Side 1 (instep) of each sock still has	30 sts	36 sts
Side 2 (sole) of each sock now has	60 sts	72 sts

Shaping the Heel Cup, Sock B

Set Up This is a partial round, worked only on side 1 (instep) of both socks.
- **SIDE 1 (INSTEP), socks A and B:** Work the Simplicity Chart as established.
- **ROTATE:** Rotate work and arrange stitches so that you are ready to begin working the heel on side 2 of sock B.

NOTE While shaping the heel cup and working the heel flap, you temporarily switch to working the socks individually. You first work side 2 of sock B back and forth in short rows, then you work side 2 of sock A in a similar manner. When the heels are completed, you return to knitting the socks together in rounds (in the Knitting the Legs section below). For information about short rows and wrapping stitches, see Tips for Shaping the Heel (page 34).

Side 2, Row 1 (right side)
- Knit   ⑤ 15 sts   ⓛ 18 sts
- Place marker 1.
- Knit   ⑤ 29 sts   ⓛ 35 sts
- Slip 1 as if to purl, bring yarn to the right side to wrap stitch, place marker 2 on left-hand needle, slip stitch back to left-hand needle. Turn work to the wrong side.

Side 2, Row 2 (wrong side) Purl to 1 stitch before marker 1, slip 1 as if to purl, bring yarn to right side to wrap stitch, slip stitch back to left-hand needle. Turn work to the right side.

Side 2, Row 3 (right side) Knit to 2 stitches before previously wrapped stitch, slip 1 as if to purl, bring yarn to right side to wrap stitch, slip stitch back to left-hand needle. Turn.

Side 2, Row 4 (wrong side) Purl to 2 stitches before previously wrapped stitch, slip 1 as if to purl, bring yarn to right side to wrap stitch, slip stitch back to left-hand needle. Turn.

Next Rows Repeat Rows 3 and 4 until all but the 4 center stitches have been wrapped. End having just completed   ⑤ Row 4   ⓛ Row 3

For Adult's Small Only

Next Row Knit 3 stitches, slip 1 as if to purl, bring yarn to right side to wrap stitch, slip stitch back to left-hand needle. Turn.

Working the Heel Flap, Sock B

NOTE Continue to work back and forth in rows on side 2, sock B only. During the first two rows of the heel flap, you will be lifting and working the wraps that you created in the heel-cup shaping steps above. For information on lifting and working wraps on the right and wrong side, see Tips for Working Wrapped Stitches (page 38).

Side 2, Row 1 (wrong side)   Purl, lifting the wraps and purling them together with their respective stitches as you come to them, to 1 stitch before marker 1. Then, lift the wrap of the stitch before marker 1, slip both stitch and wrap to the right-hand needle as if to purl, remove marker, slip both stitch and wrap back to the left-hand needle, and purl together the wrap and its stitch along with the next stitch (P3tog). Turn.

Side 2, Row 2 (right side)   Slip 1 as if to purl. Then knit, lifting the wraps and knitting them together with their respective stitches as you come to them, to 1 stitch before marker 2. Lift the wrap of the next stitch completely over and to the left of the stitch, slip the stitch as if to knit, slip the wrap as if to knit, remove marker, slip next stitch as if to knit, place the 2 slipped stitches and the wrap back on left-hand needle, and knit the 2 slipped stitches together with the wrap through the back loop. Turn.

Side 2, Row 3 (wrong side)   Slip 1 as if to purl, purl to 1 stitch before gap, P2tog to close gap. Turn.

NOTE From this point on, this heel flap is worked in Eye-of-Partridge Stitch (as written out in Rows 4–7) with a 2-stitch garter-stitch border and 1 edge stitch on each side.

Side 2, Row 4 (right side)   Slip 1 as if to purl, K2, *slip 1, K1; repeat from * to 3 stitches before gap, K2, ssk to close gap. Turn.

Side 2, Row 5 (wrong side)   Slip 1 as if to purl, K2, purl to 3 stitches before gap, K2, P2tog to close gap. Turn.

Side 2, Row 6 (right side)   Slip 1 as if to purl, K2, *K1, slip 1; repeat from * to 3 stitches before gap, K2, ssk to close gap. Turn.

Side 2, Row 7 (wrong side)   Slip 1 as if to purl, K2, purl to 3 stitches before gap, K2, P2tog to close gap. Turn.

Next Rows   Repeat Rows 4–7 until you have decreased away all of the gusset stitches on side 2 of this sock. End having completed a right-side row.
• Side 2 of sock B now again has   S   30 sts   L   36 sts

Shaping the Heel Cup and Working the Heel Flap, Sock A

To shape the heel cup and work the heel flap of sock A, repeat the instructions for sock B above.

Knitting the Legs

In this section you return to working in the round on all stitches for both socks.

NOTE Pick up an extra stitch at the point where the heel and instep meet to prevent holes from developing. (See Knitting the Legs, pages 41–42.)

Next Round
- **SIDE 1 (INSTEP), socks A and B:** Work across instep stitches according to the Simplicity Chart as established.
- **SIDE 2 (SOLE), socks B and A:** Work these stitches according to the Simplicity Chart, following the same row in the chart that you used on side 1.

Next Rounds Continue working in the round, following the Simplicity Chart, until the leg measurement from the top of the heel flap is

S 5" (12.5 cm)   **L** 5½" (14 cm)

Next Rounds Work in K1, P1 rib on all stitches until ribbing measures 2" (5 cm). For the large size, the ribbing lines up more closely with the stitch pattern on the leg if you start with a purl stitch.

Finishing

Loosely bind off all stitches using your preferred method (see Bind Offs, pages 159–160). Weave in loose tails. Block.

Simplicity Chart for Size Small

•		V		•	2
•				•	1

5 4 3 2 1

Key

□	Knit
•	Purl
V	Slip stitch as if to purl with yarn in back

Simplicity Chart for Size Large

•	•			•	2
•	•	V		•	1

6 5 4 3 2 1

Key

□	Knit
•	Purl
V	Slip stitch as if to purl with yarn in back

The Keep

Crenellation is the name for the jagged patterns that frame the tops of the walls of many medieval keeps and castles. It is reflected here in the angular lines of this design. These socks are keepers, for sure, and not just because of the beauty of the stitch pattern. Knitted in the stunning and delicious Malabrigo Sock, these are socks that, once knitted, you won't be letting go of any time soon.

ADULT'S SIZES	SMALL	LARGE
FINISHED FOOT CIRCUMFERENCE	6¾" (17 cm)	7¾" (19.5 cm)
YARN	Malabrigo Sock, 100% superwash merino, 3.5 oz (100 g)/440 yds (402 m) [*Yarn band gauge: 8 stitches = 1" (2.5 cm) on US 0–1 (2.0–2.25 mm) needles*]; Velvet Grapes: 1 skein	
GAUGE	10 stitches and 12 rows = 1" (2.5 cm) in stockinette stitch	
NEEDLE	US 0 (2.0 mm) 40" (100 cm) circular, *or size needed to obtain correct gauge*	
NOTIONS	3 stitch markers (including 1 locking stitch marker), darning needle	

Pattern Stitches

Stockinette
Knit every round.

The Keep
See The Keep Charts on page 127.

Casting On and Shaping the Toes

Cast On   Follow the instructions for casting on stitches on pages 23–26 to cast on 16 stitches for sock B and 16 stitches for sock A.

Round 1   Follow the instructions for knitting Round 1 on pages 27–30 to knit the first round on both socks. You now have 8 stitches on side 1 (instep) for each sock and 8 stitches on side 2 (sole) for each sock.

Round 2 (increase)

NOTE All make 1 (M1) increases should be worked with a backward loop increase (see Backward Loop Increases on page 159).

- **SIDE 1 (INSTEP), sock A:** K1, M1R, knit to 1 stitch before the end, M1L, K1.
- **SIDE 1 (INSTEP), sock B:** K1, M1R, knit to 1 stitch before the end, M1L, K1.
- **ROTATE:** Rotate your work and arrange your stitches on the needles so that you are ready to work the sole stitches on side 2 of both socks.
- **SIDE 2 (SOLE), socks B and A:** Repeat the side 1 increases on both socks.
- Each sock now has 20 stitches (10 on each side of each sock).
- **ROTATE:** Rotate your work and arrange stitches so that you are ready to begin the next round.

Next Rounds
- Work Round 2 increases   S 6 more times   L 7 more times
- Each sock now has   S 44 sts   L 48 sts

Next Round (even)   Knit both sides of socks A and B with no increases.

Next Round (increase)   Repeat Round 2.

Next Rounds
- Repeat the last 2 rounds (knit even and increase)
                                  S 6 more times   L 8 more times
- End your work back at the marker having just finished side 2, sock A.
- Each sock now has a total of   S 72 sts   L 84 sts
- Each side of each sock now has S 36 sts   L 42 sts

Knitting the Feet

Round 1
- **SIDE 1 (INSTEP), socks A and B:** Work The Keep Chart, beginning at the lower right.
- **SIDE 2 (SOLE), socks B and A:** Knit to end (stockinette stitch).

Next Rounds Repeat the previous round, continuing to work The Keep Chart on side 1 of each sock and keeping side 2 in stockinette, until the socks measure the appropriate length (see Toe-to-Gusset Length, above). End your work having just finished side 2, sock A. You are back at your marker and ready to begin the gusset increases.

> ### TOE-TO-GUSSET LENGTH
> Use this handy formula. Note: For Z, measure on side 2 of sock.
>
> $\mathbf{X}$ (desired total sock length) = _____"
> $\mathbf{Y}$ (# of rows in gusset and heel cup) = 53 (S); 63 (L)
> $\mathbf{Z}$ (rows per inch) = _____
> $\mathbf{TGL}$ (toe-to-gusset length) = _____"
>
> $$\underbrace{\rule{2cm}{0.4pt}}_{X}{}'' - (\underbrace{\rule{1.5cm}{0.4pt}}_{Y} \div \underbrace{\rule{1.5cm}{0.4pt}}_{Z}) = \underbrace{\rule{2cm}{0.4pt}}_{TGL}{}''$$
>
> For more information, see Toe-Up Math, page 19.

Increasing for the Gussets

Round 1 (increase)
- **SIDE 1 (INSTEP), socks A and B:** Continue to work The Keep Chart as established.
- **SIDE 2 (SOLE), socks B and A:** K1, M1R, knit to last stitch of each sock, M1L, K1.

Round 2 (even)
- **SIDE 1 (INSTEP), socks A and B:** Continue to work The Keep Chart as established.
- **SIDE 2 (SOLE), socks B and A:** Work in stockinette stitch as established.

Next Rounds
- Repeat Rounds 1 and 2   Ⓢ 17 more times   Ⓛ 20 more times
- Side 1 (instep) of each sock still has   Ⓢ 36 sts   Ⓛ 42 sts
- Side 2 (sole) of each sock now has   Ⓢ 72 sts   Ⓛ 84 sts

Shaping the Heel Cup, Sock B

Set Up   This is a partial round, worked only on side 1 (instep) of both socks.
- SIDE 1 (INSTEP), **socks A and B:** Work The Keep Chart as established.
- ROTATE: Rotate work and arrange stitches so that you are ready to begin working the heel on side 2 of sock B.

NOTE   While shaping the heel cup and working the heel flap, you temporarily switch to working the socks individually. You first work side 2 of sock B back and forth in short rows, then you work side 2 of sock A in a similar manner. When the heels are completed, you return to knitting the socks together in rounds (in the Knitting the Legs section below). For information about short rows and wrapping stitches, see Tips for Shaping the Heel (page 34).

Side 2, Row 1 (right side)
- Knit   **S** 18 sts   **L** 21 sts
- Place marker 1.
- Knit   **S** 35 sts   **L** 41 sts
- Slip 1 as if to purl, bring yarn to the right side to wrap stitch, place marker 2 on left-hand needle, slip stitch back to left-hand needle. Turn work to the wrong side.

Side 2, Row 2 (wrong side)   Purl to 1 stitch before marker 1, slip 1 as if to purl, bring yarn to right side to wrap stitch, slip stitch back to left-hand needle. Turn work to the right side.

Side 2, Row 3 (right side)   Knit to 2 stitches before previously wrapped stitch, slip 1 as if to purl, bring yarn to right side to wrap stitch, slip stitch back to left-hand needle. Turn.

Side 2, Row 4 (wrong side)   Purl to 2 stitches before previously wrapped stitch, slip 1 as if to purl, bring yarn to right side to wrap stitch, slip stitch back to left-hand needle. Turn.

Next Rows   Repeat Rows 3 and 4 until all but the 4 center stitches have been wrapped. End having just completed   **S** Row 3   **L** Row 4

For Adult's Large Only

Next Row   Knit 3 stitches, slip 1 as if to purl, bring yarn to right side to wrap stitch, slip stitch back to left-hand needle. Turn.

Working the Heel Flap, Sock B

NOTE Continue to work back and forth in rows on side 2, sock B only. During the first two rows of the heel flap, you will be lifting and working the wraps that you created in the heel-cup shaping steps above. For information on lifting and working wraps on the right and wrong side, see Tips for Working Wrapped Stitches (page 38).

Side 2, Row 1 (wrong side) Purl, lifting the wraps and purling them together with their respective stitches as you come to them, to 1 stitch before marker 1. Then, lift the wrap of the stitch before marker 1, slip both stitch and wrap to the right-hand needle as if to purl, remove marker, slip both stitch and wrap back to the left-hand needle, and purl together the wrap and its stitch along with the next stitch (P3tog). Turn.

Side 2, Row 2 (right side) Slip 1 as if to purl. Then knit, lifting the wraps and knitting them together with their respective stitches as you come to them, to 1 stitch before marker 2. Lift the wrap of the next stitch completely over and to the left of the stitch, slip the stitch as if to knit, slip the wrap as if to knit, remove marker, slip next stitch as if to knit, place the 2 slipped stitches and the wrap back on left-hand needle, and knit the 2 slipped stitches together with the wrap through the back loop. Turn.

Side 2, Row 3 (wrong side) Slip 1 as if to purl, purl to 1 stitch before gap, P2tog to close gap. Turn.

Side 2, Row 4 (right side) Slip 1 as if to purl, *K1, slip 1 as if to purl; repeat from * to 1 stitch before gap, ssk to close gap. Turn.

Side 2, Row 5 (wrong side) Slip 1 as if to purl, purl to 1 stitch before gap, P2tog to close gap. Turn.

Next Rows Repeat Rows 4 and 5 until you have decreased away all of the gusset stitches on side 2 of this sock. End having completed a right-side row.
• Side 2 of sock B now again has   **S** 36 sts   **L** 42 sts

Shaping the Heel Cup and Working the Heel Flap, Sock A

To shape the heel cup and work the heel flap of sock A, repeat the instructions for sock B above.

Knitting the Legs

In this section you return to working in the round on all stitches for both socks.

NOTE Pick up an extra stitch at the point where the heel and instep meet to prevent holes from developing. (See Knitting the Legs, pages 41–42.)

Next Round
- SIDE 1 (INSTEP), **socks A and B:** Work across instep stitches according to The Keep Chart as established.
- SIDE 2 (SOLE), **socks B and A:** Work these stitches according to The Keep Chart, following the same row in the chart that you used on side 1.

Next Rounds   Continue working in the round, following The Keep Chart for all stitches, until the leg measurement from the top of the heel flap is 4" (10 cm).

Next Rounds   Work stockinette stitch on all stitches for 1" (2.5 cm).

Finishing

Loosely bind off all stitches using your preferred method (see Bind Offs, pages 159–160). Weave in loose tails. Block.

The Keep Chart for Size Small

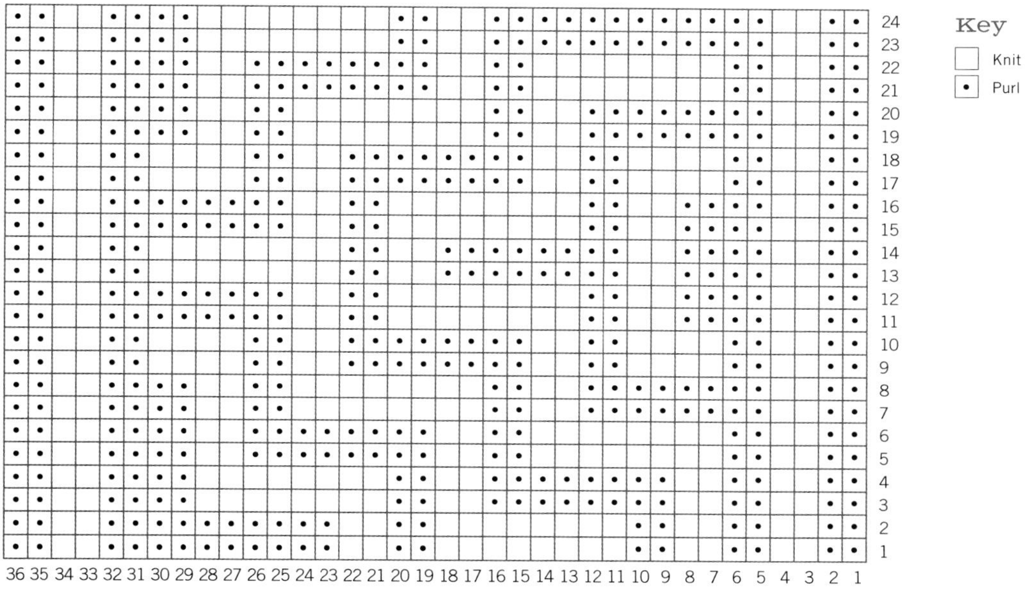
Key
Knit
Purl

The Keep Chart for Size Large

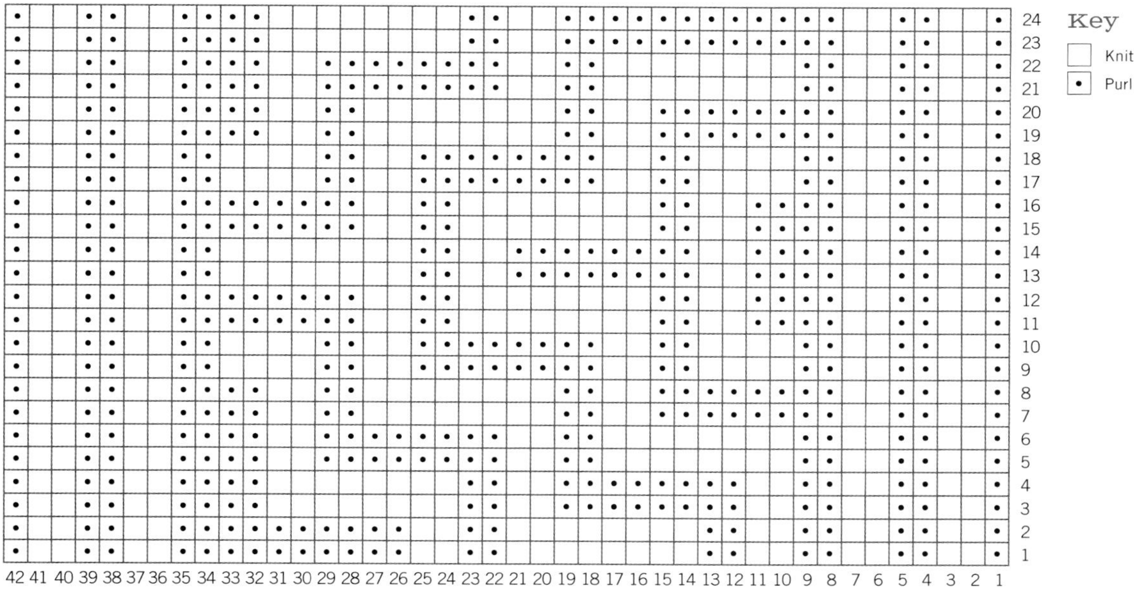
Key
Knit
Purl

Raindrops

Worked in the elegant Schaefer Heather, this stitch pattern catches the light reflected by this yarn's perfect percentage of silk. Do you know how rain rolls lazily down a window in the spring, leaving a trail behind it? That's what this pattern reminds me of: spring rain trickling down my windows, leaving tiny shimmering beads along its path.

ADULT'S SIZES	SMALL	LARGE
FINISHED FOOT CIRCUMFERENCE	6½" (16.5 cm)	7½" (19 cm)
YARN	Schaefer Yarn Heather, 55% merino wool superwash/30% cultivated silk/15% nylon, 4 oz (114 g)/400 yds (366 m) [*Yarn band gauge: 7–8 stitches = 1" (2.5 cm) in stockinette stitch on US 1 (2.25.mm) needles*]; Sage: 1 skein	
GAUGE	7 stitches and 9 rows = 1" (2.5 cm) in stockinette stitch	
NEEDLE	US 2 (2.75 mm) 40" (100 cm) circular, *or size needed to obtain correct gauge*	
NOTIONS	3 stitch markers (including 1 locking stitch marker), darning needle	

Pattern Stitches

Raindrops (multiple of 8)
See the Raindrops Chart on page 135.

Ribbing
*K1,P1; repeat from *.

Stockinette
Knit every round.

Casting On and Shaping the Toes

Cast On   Follow the instructions for casting on stitches on pages 23–26 to cast on 12 stitches for sock B and 12 stitches for sock A.

Round 1   Follow the instructions for knitting Round 1 on pages 27–30 to knit the first round on both socks. You now have 6 stitches on side 1 (instep) for each sock and 6 stitches on side 2 (sole) for each sock.

Round 2 (increase)

> **NOTE** All make 1 (M1) increases should be worked with a backward loop increase (see Backward Loop Increases on page 159).

- **SIDE 1 (INSTEP), sock A:** K1, M1R, knit to 1 stitch before the end, M1L, K1.
- **SIDE 1 (INSTEP), sock B:** K1, M1R, knit to 1 stitch before the end, M1L, K1.
- **ROTATE:** Rotate your work and arrange your stitches on the needles so that you are ready to work the sole stitches on side 2 of both socks.
- **SIDE 2 (SOLE), socks B and A:** Repeat the side 1 increases on both socks.
- Each sock now has 16 stitches (8 on each side of each sock).
- **ROTATE:** Rotate your work and arrange stitches so that you are ready to begin the next round.

Next Rounds

- Work Round 2 increases   S 4 more times   L 5 more times
- Each sock now has   S 32 sts   L 36 sts

Next Round (even)   Knit both sides of socks A and B with no increases.

Next Round (increase)   Repeat Round 2.

Next Rounds

- Repeat the last 2 rounds (knit even and increase)
     S 5 more times   L 6 more times
- End your work back at the marker having just finished side 2, sock A.
- Each sock now has a total of   S 56 sts   L 64 sts
- Each side of each sock now has   S 28 sts   L 32 sts

Knitting the Feet

Round 1
- **SIDE 1 (INSTEP), socks A and B:** Work K1, P1 ribbing on all stitches.
- **SIDE 2 (SOLE), socks B and A:** Work K1, P1 ribbing on all stitches.

Next Rounds Repeat the previous round, continuing to work the K1, P1 ribbing until the socks measure the appropriate length (see Toe-to-Gusset Length, above). End your work having just finished side 2, sock A. You are back at your marker and ready to begin the gusset increases.

> ### TOE-TO-GUSSET LENGTH
> Use this handy formula. Note: For Z, measure on side 2 of sock.
>
> | | | |
> |---|---|---|
> | **X** | (desired total sock length) | = _____ " |
> | **Y** | (# of rows in gusset and heel cup) | = 41 (S); 47 (L) |
> | **Z** | (rows per inch) | = _____ |
> | **TGL** | (toe-to-gusset length) | = _____ " |
>
> $$\frac{\underline{\quad}"}{X} - \left(\frac{\underline{\quad}}{Y} \div \underline{\quad}_{Z}\right) = \underline{\quad}"_{TGL}$$
>
> For more information, see Toe-Up Math, page 19.

Increasing for the Gussets

Round 1 (increase)
- **SIDE 1 (INSTEP), socks A and B:** Continue to work K1, P1 ribbing as established.
- **SIDE 2 (SOLE), socks B and A:** K1, M1R, work in ribbing as established to last stitch of each sock, M1L, P1.

Round 2 (even)
- **SIDE 1 (INSTEP), socks A and B:** Continue to work K1, P1 ribbing as established.
- **SIDE 2 (SOLE), socks B and A:** Work in ribbing as established, keeping the first stitch of each sock as a knit stitch and the last stitch of each sock as a purl stitch. The M1 stitches from the previous round should be incorporated into the rib pattern.

Next Rounds
- Repeat Rounds 1 and 2
- Side 1 (instep) of each sock still has
- Side 2 (sole) of each sock now has

ⓢ 13 more times
ⓢ 28 sts
ⓢ 56 sts

Ⓛ 15 more times
Ⓛ 32 sts
Ⓛ 64 sts

Shaping the Heel Cup, Sock B

Set Up This is a partial round, worked only on side 1 (instep) of both socks.
- **SIDE 1 (INSTEP), socks A and B:** Work K1, P1 rib as established.
- **ROTATE:** Rotate work and arrange stitches so that you are ready to begin working the heel on side 2 of sock B.

NOTE While shaping the heel cup and working the heel flap, you temporarily switch to working the socks individually. You first work side 2 of sock B back and forth in short rows, then you work side 2 of sock A in a similar manner. When the heels are completed, you return to knitting the socks together in rounds (in the Knitting the Legs section below). For information about short rows and wrapping stitches, see Tips for Shaping the Heel (page 34).

Side 2, Row 1 (right side)
- Knit   S 14 sts   L 16 sts
- Place marker 1.
- Knit   S 27 sts   L 31 sts
- Slip 1 as if to purl, bring yarn to the right side to wrap stitch, place marker 2 on left-hand needle, slip stitch back to left-hand needle. Turn work to the wrong side.

Side 2, Row 2 (wrong side) Purl to 1 stitch before marker 1, slip 1 as if to purl, bring yarn to right side to wrap stitch, slip stitch back to left-hand needle. Turn work to the right side.

Side 2, Row 3 (right side) Knit to 2 stitches before previously wrapped stitch, slip 1 as if to purl, bring yarn to right side to wrap stitch, slip stitch back to left-hand needle. Turn.

Side 2, Row 4 (wrong side) Purl to 2 stitches before previously wrapped stitch, slip 1 as if to purl, bring yarn to right side to wrap stitch, slip stitch back to left-hand needle. Turn.

Next Rows Repeat Rows 3 and 4 until all but the 4 center stitches have been wrapped. End having just completed Row 3.

Working the Heel Flap, Sock B

NOTE Continue to work back and forth in rows on side 2, sock B only. During the first two rows of the heel flap, you will be lifting and working the wraps that you created in the heel-cup shaping steps above. For information on lifting and working wraps on the right and wrong side, see Tips for Working Wrapped Stitches (page 38).

Side 2, Row 1 (wrong side) Purl, lifting the wraps and purling them together with their respective stitches as you come to them, to 1 stitch before marker 1. Then, lift the wrap of the stitch before marker 1, slip both stitch and wrap to the right-hand needle as if to purl, remove marker, slip both stitch and wrap back to the left-hand needle, and purl together the wrap and its stitch along with the next stitch (P3tog). Turn.

Side 2, Row 2 (right side) Slip 1 as if to purl. Then knit, lifting the wraps and knitting them together with their respective stitches as you come to them, to 1 stitch before marker 2. Lift the wrap of the next stitch completely over and to the left of the stitch, slip the stitch as if to knit, slip the wrap as if to knit, remove marker, slip next stitch as if to knit, place the 2 slipped stitches and the wrap back on left-hand needle, and knit the 2 slipped stitches together with the wrap through the back loop. Turn.

Side 2, Row 3 (wrong side) Slip 1 as if to purl, purl to 1 stitch before gap, P2tog to close gap. Turn.

Side 2, Row 4 (right side) Slip 1 as if to purl, *K1, slip 1 as if to purl; repeat from * to 1 stitch before gap, ssk to close gap. Turn.

Side 2, Row 5 (wrong side) Slip 1 as if to purl, purl to 1 stitch before gap, P2tog to close gap. Turn.

Next Rows Repeat Rows 4 and 5 until you have decreased away all of the gusset stitches on side 2 of this sock. End having completed a right-side row.

• Side 2 of sock B now again has   **S** 28 sts   **L** 32 sts

Shaping the Heel Cup and Working the Heel Flap, Sock A

To shape the heel cup and work the heel flap of sock A, repeat the instructions for sock B above.

Knitting the Legs

In this section you return to working in the round on all stitches for both socks.

NOTE Pick up an extra stitch at the point where the heel and instep meet to prevent holes from developing. (See Knitting the Legs, pages 41–42.)

Next Round
- SIDE 1 (INSTEP), **socks A and B:** Work across instep stitches according to the Raindrops Chart, beginning at the lower right. If you are knitting the small size, there will only be three-and-a-half repeats of the stitch pattern on each side of each sock; if you are knitting the large size, work four full repeats.
- SIDE 2 (SOLE), **socks B and A:** Work these stitches according to the Raindrops Chart, beginning at the lower right. When working side 2, make sure you begin with the column in the chart that you left off with on side 1 (column 5).

Next Rounds Continue working in the round, following the Raindrops Chart for all stitches, until the leg measurement from the top of the heel flap is approximately 5½" (14 cm). You can end with any row in the Raindrops Chart, but it may look best if you don't end with Rows 3–7 (the yarn over rows).

Next Rounds Work K1, P1 ribbing on all stitches for 1" (2.5 cm).

Finishing

Loosely bind off all stitches using your preferred method (see Bind Offs, pages 159–160). Weave in loose tails. Block.

Raindrops Chart

8	7	6	5	4	3	2	1	
•	•	•	•	•	•	•	•	20
•	•	•	•	•	•	•	•	19
•	•	•	•	•	•	•		18
•	•	•	•	•	•	•		17
•		•	•	•		•		16
•		•	•	•		•		15
•		•		•		•		14
•		•		•		•		13
•		•		•		•		12
•		•		•		•		11
•		•		•		•		10
•		•		•		•		9
•		•		•		•		8
•		•		•		/.	O	7
•		•		•		•		6
/.	O	•		/.	O	•	•	5
•	•	•		•	•	•	•	4
•	•	/.	O	•	•	•	•	3
•	•	•	•	•	•	•	•	2
•	•	•	•	•	•	•	•	1

Key

☐	Knit
•	Purl
O	Yarn over
/.	Purl 2 together

Wavelength

The yarn used in these kids' socks is called "rainbow dyed" on the company's Web site, and I agree! This pattern works very well with any striping yarn because it lets the yarn "make waves." This also might be a great way to use up small bits of leftover sock yarns, changing colors every half-inch or so. Whatever yarn you choose, there's fun to be found in waves of all kinds!

CHILD'S SIZES	SMALL	LARGE
FINISHED FOOT CIRCUMFERENCE	5" (12.5 cm)	6¼" (16 cm)
YARN	Knit One, Crochet Too Ty-Dy Socks, 80% superwash wool/20% nylon, 3.5 oz (100 g)/436 yds (399 m) [*Yarn band gauge: 8½ stitches = 1" (2.5 cm) in stockinette stitch on US 1 (2.25 mm) needles*]; Blue Pansy 1672: 1 skein	
GAUGE	8 stitches and 11 rows = 1" (2.5 cm) in stockinette stitch	
NEEDLE	US 1 (2.25 mm) 40" (100 cm) circular, *or size needed to obtain correct gauge*	
NOTIONS	3 stitch markers (including 1 locking stitch marker), darning needle	

Pattern Stitches

Wavelength (multiple of 6)
See the Wavelength Chart on page 142.
Round 1: *K1, yo, ssk, K2tog, yo, K1; repeat from *.
Round 2: Knit.

Ribbing
*K1,P1; repeat from *.

Stockinette
Knit every round.

Casting On and Shaping the Toes

Cast On   Follow the instructions for casting on stitches on pages 23–26 to cast on 12 stitches for sock B and 12 stitches for sock A.

Round 1   Follow the instructions for knitting Round 1 on pages 27–30 to knit the first round on both socks. You now have 6 stitches on side 1 (instep) for each sock and 6 stitches on side 2 (sole) for each sock.

Round 2 (increase)

> NOTE   All make 1 (M1) increases should be worked with a backward loop increase (see Backward Loop Increases on page 159).

- **SIDE 1** (INSTEP), **sock A:** K1, M1R, knit to 1 stitch before the end, M1L, K1.
- **SIDE 1** (INSTEP), **sock B:** K1, M1R, knit to 1 stitch before the end, M1L, K1.
- **ROTATE:** Rotate your work and arrange your stitches on the needles so that you are ready to work the sole stitches on side 2 of both socks.
- **SIDE 2** (SOLE), **socks B and A:** Repeat the side 1 increases on both socks.
- Each sock now has 16 stitches (8 on each side of each sock).
- **ROTATE:** Rotate your work and arrange stitches so that you are ready to begin the next round.

Next Rounds

• Work Round 2 increases	**S** 3 more times	**L** 5 more times
• Each sock now has a total of	**S** 28 sts	**L** 36 sts

Next Round (even)   Knit both sides of socks A and B with no increases.

Next Round (increase)   Repeat Round 2.

Next Rounds

- Repeat the last 2 rounds (knit even and increase)

	S 4 more times	**L** 5 more times

- End your work back at the marker having just finished side 2, sock A.

• Each sock now has	**S** 48 sts	**L** 60 sts
• Each side of each sock now has	**S** 24 sts	**L** 30 sts

Knitting the Feet

Round 1

- **SIDE 1** (INSTEP), **socks A and B:** Work the Wavelength Chart, beginning at the lower right.
- **SIDE 2** (SOLE), **socks B and A:** Knit to end (stockinette stitch).

Next Rounds Repeat the previous round, continuing to work the Wavelength Chart on side 1 of each sock and keeping side 2 in stockinette stitch, until the socks measure the appropriate length (see Toe-to-Gusset Length, above). End your work having just finished side 2, sock A. You are back at your marker to begin the gusset increases.

TOE-TO-GUSSET LENGTH

Use this handy formula. Note: For Z, measure on side 2 of sock.

X (desired total sock length) = _____ "
Y (# of rows in gusset and heel cup) = 35 (S); 45 (L)
Z (rows per inch) = _____
TGL (toe-to-gusset length) = _____ "

$$\underline{\hspace{2cm}}^{"} - (\underline{\hspace{2cm}} \div \underline{\hspace{2cm}}) = \underline{\hspace{2cm}}^{"}$$
$$\quad X \qquad\qquad Y \qquad Z \qquad\quad TGL$$

For more information, see Toe-Up Math, page 19.

Increasing for the Gussets

Round 1 (increase)

- **SIDE 1** (INSTEP), **socks A and B:** Continue to work the Wavelength Chart as established.
- **SIDE 2** (SOLE), **socks B and A:** K1, M1R, knit to last stitch of each sock M1L, K1.

Round 2 (even)

- **SIDE 1** (INSTEP), **socks A and B:** Continue to work the Wavelength Chart as established.
- **SIDE 2** (SOLE), **socks B and A:** Work in stockinette stitch as established.

Next Rounds

	S	L
• Repeat Rounds 1 and 2	11 more times	14 more times
• Side 1 (instep) of each sock still has	24 sts	30 sts
• Side 2 (sole) of each sock now has	48 sts	60 sts

Shaping the Heel Cup, Sock B

Set Up This is a partial round, worked only on side 1 (instep) of both socks.
- **SIDE 1** (INSTEP), **socks A and B:** Work the Wavelength Chart as established.
- **ROTATE:** Rotate work and arrange stitches so that you are ready to begin working the heel on side 2 of sock B.

> **NOTE** While shaping the heel cup and working the heel flap, you temporarily switch to working the socks individually. You first work side 2 of sock B back and forth in short rows, then you work side 2 of sock A in a similar manner. When the heels are completed, you return to knitting the socks together in rounds (in the Knitting the Legs section, below). For information about short rows and wrapping stitches, see Tips for Shaping the Heel (page 34).

Side 2, Row 1 (right side)
- Knit   Ⓢ 12 sts   Ⓛ 15 sts
- Place marker 1.
- Knit   Ⓢ 23 sts   Ⓛ 29 sts
- Slip 1 as if to purl, bring yarn to the right side to wrap stitch, place marker 2 on left-hand needle, slip stitch back to left-hand needle. Turn work to the wrong side.

Side 2, Row 2 (wrong side)
Purl to 1 stitch before marker 1, slip 1 as if to purl, bring yarn to right side to wrap stitch, slip stitch back to left-hand needle. Turn work to the right side.

Side 2, Row 3 (right side)
Knit to 2 stitches before previously wrapped stitch, slip 1 as if to purl, bring yarn to right side to wrap stitch, slip stitch back to left-hand needle. Turn.

Side 2, Row 4 (wrong side)
Purl to 2 stitches before previously wrapped stitch, slip 1 as if to purl, bring yarn to right side to wrap stitch, slip stitch back to left-hand needle. Turn.

Next Rows Repeat Rows 3 and 4 until all but the 4 center stitches have been wrapped. End having just completed   Ⓢ Row 3   Ⓛ Row 4

For Child's Large Only

Next Row Knit 3 stitches, slip 1 as if to purl, bring yarn to right side to wrap stitch, slip stitch back to left-hand needle. Turn.

S Small   L Large

Working the Heel Flap, Sock B

NOTE Continue to work back and forth in rows on side 2, sock B only. During the first two rows of the heel flap, you will be lifting and working the wraps that you created in the heel-cup shaping steps above. For information on lifting and working wraps on the right and wrong side, see Tips for Working Wrapped Stitches (page 38).

Side 2, Row 1 (wrong side) Purl, lifting the wraps and purling them together with their respective stitches as you come to them, to 1 stitch before marker 1. Then, lift the wrap of the stitch before marker 1, slip both stitch and wrap to the right-hand needle as if to purl, remove marker, slip both stitch and wrap back to the left-hand needle, and purl together the wrap and its stitch along with the next stitch (P3tog). Turn.

Side 2, Row 2 (right side) Slip 1 as if to purl. Then knit, lifting the wraps and knitting them together with their respective stitches as you come to them, to 1 stitch before marker 2. Lift the wrap of the next stitch completely over and to the left of the stitch, slip the stitch as if to knit, slip the wrap as if to knit, remove marker, slip next stitch as if to knit, place the 2 slipped stitches and the wrap back on left-hand needle, and knit the 2 slipped stitches together with the wrap through the back loop. Turn.

Side 2, Row 3 (wrong side) Slip 1 as if to purl, purl to 1 stitch before gap, P2tog to close gap. Turn.

Side 2, Row 4 (right side) Slip 1 as if to purl, *K1, slip 1 as if to purl; repeat from * to 1 stitch before gap, ssk to close gap. Turn.

Side 2, Row 5 (wrong side) Slip 1 as if to purl, purl to 1 stitch before gap, P2tog to close gap. Turn.

Next Rows Repeat Rows 4 and 5 until you have decreased away all of the gusset stitches on side 2 of this sock. End having completed a right-side row.
 • Side 2 of sock B now again has   S 24 sts   L 30 sts

Shaping the Heel Cup and Working the Heel Flap, Sock A

To shape the heel cup and work the heel flap of sock A, repeat the instructions for sock B above.

Knitting the Legs

In this section you return to working in the round on all stitches for both socks.

NOTE Pick up an extra stitch at the point where the heel and instep meet to prevent holes from developing. (See Knitting the Legs, pages 41–42.)

Next Round
- SIDE 1 (INSTEP), **socks A and B:** Work across instep stitches according to the Wavelength Chart as established.
- SIDE 2 (SOLE), **socks B and A:** Work these stitches according to the Wavelength Chart, following the same row in the chart that you used on side 1.

Next Rounds Continue working in the round, following the Wavelength Chart for all stitches, until the leg measurement from the top of the heel flap is

S 2" (5 cm)   L 2½" (6.4 cm)

Next Rounds Work K1, P1 rib for 1½" (3.75 cm).

Finishing

Loosely bind off all stitches using your preferred method (see Bind Offs, pages 159–160). Weave in loose tails. Block.

Wavelength Chart

	o	/	\	o		2
						1

6 5 4 3 2 1

Key
- ☐ Knit
- o Yarn over
- \ Slip, slip, knit
- / Knit 2 together

Peppercorn

Tiny nubs of knit stitch set off the dramatic changes in my very favorite Noro colorway. Knitted in their amazing colors or in any yarn with long color changes, these textured socks are sure to be a hit. This Noro wool can be rinsed with a natural hair conditioner after a wool-safe soap wash, if desired, for greater softness.

ADULT'S SIZES	SMALL	LARGE
FINISHED FOOT CIRCUMFERENCE	7½" (19 cm)	8½" (21.5 cm)
YARN	Noro Silk Garden Sock, 40% wool/25% silk/25% nylon/10% mohair, 3.5 oz (100 g)/330 yds (302 m) [Yarn band gauge: 8 stitches = 1" (2.5 cm) in stockinette stitch on US 2–3 (2.75–3.25 mm) needles]; Color S84: 1 skein for Small; 2 skeins for Large	
GAUGE	8 stitches and 11 rows = 1" (2.5 cm) in stockinette stitch	
NEEDLE	US 1 (2.25 mm) 40" (100 cm) circular, or size needed to obtain correct gauge	
NOTIONS	3 stitch markers (including 1 locking stitch marker), darning needle	

Pattern Stitches

Peppercorn (multiple of 4)
See the Peppercorn Chart on page 149.
Round 1: Knit.
Round 2: *K4, [slip last stitch back to left-hand needle, Ktbl] four times; repeat from *.
Round 3: Knit.
Round 4: *K2, [slip last stitch back to left-hand needle, Ktbl] four times, K2; repeat from *.

Garter
Purl 1 round, knit 1 round.

Ribbing
*K1, P1; repeat from *.

Stockinette
Knit every round.

Casting On and Shaping the Toes

Cast On   Follow the instructions for casting on stitches on pages 23–26 to cast on 12 stitches for sock B and 12 stitches for sock A.

Round 1   Follow the instructions for knitting Round 1 on pages 27–30 to knit the first round on both socks. You now have 6 stitches on side 1 (instep) for each sock and 6 stitches on side 2 (sole) for each sock.

Round 2 (increase)

NOTE   All make 1 (M1) increases should be worked with a backward loop increase (see Backward Loop Increases on page 159).

- **SIDE 1** (INSTEP), **sock A:** K1, M1R, knit to 1 stitch before the end, M1L, K1.
- **SIDE 1** (INSTEP), **sock B:** K1, M1R, knit to 1 stitch before the end, M1L, K1.
- **ROTATE:** Rotate your work and arrange your stitches on the needles so that you are ready to work the sole stitches on side 2 of both socks.
- **SIDE 2** (SOLE), **socks B and A:** Repeat the side 1 increases on both socks.
- Each sock now has 16 stitches (8 on each side of each sock).
- **ROTATE:** Rotate your work and arrange stitches so that you are ready to begin the next round.

Next Rounds
- Work Round 2 increases   **S** 6 more times   **L** 7 more times
- Each sock now has   **S** 40 sts   **L** 44 sts

Next Round (even)   Knit both sides of socks A and B with no increases.

Next Round (increase)   Repeat Round 2.

Next Rounds
- Repeat the last 2 rounds (knit even and increase)
                                  S 5 more times   **L** 6 more times
- End your work back at the marker having just finished side 2, sock A.
- Each sock now has a total of   **S** 64 sts   **L** 72 sts
- Each side of each sock now has **S** 32 sts   **L** 36 sts

Knitting the Feet

Round 1
- **SIDE 1 (INSTEP), socks A and B:** Work the Peppercorn Chart, beginning at the lower right.
- **SIDE 2 (SOLE), socks B and A:** Knit to end (stockinette stitch).

Next Rounds Repeat the previous round, continuing to work the Peppercorn Chart on side 1 of each sock and keeping side 2 in stockinette, until the socks measure the appropriate length (see Toe-to-Gusset Length, above). End your work having just finished side 2, sock A. You are back at your marker and ready to begin the gusset increases.

> ## TOE-TO-GUSSET LENGTH
>
> Use this handy formula. Note: For Z, measure on side 2 of sock.
>
> **X** (desired total sock length) = _____"
> **Y** (# of rows in gusset and heel cup) = 47 (S); 53 (L)
> **Z** (rows per inch) = _____
> **TGL** (toe-to-gusset length) = _____"
>
> $$\underline{\qquad}" - (\underline{\qquad} \div \underline{\qquad}) = \underline{\qquad}"$$
> $$\quad\text{X} \qquad\quad \text{Y} \qquad \text{Z} \qquad\quad \text{TGL}$$
>
> For more information, see Toe-Up Math, page 19.

Increasing for the Gussets

Round 1 (increase)
- **SIDE 1 (INSTEP), socks A and B:** Continue to work the Peppercorn Chart as established.
- **SIDE 2 (SOLE), socks B and A:** K1, M1R, knit to last stitch of each sock, M1L, K1.

Round 2 (even)
- **SIDE 1 (INSTEP), socks A and B:** Continue to work the Peppercorn Chart as established.
- **SIDE 2 (SOLE), socks B and A:** Work in stockinette stitch as established.

Next Rounds
- Repeat Rounds 1 and 2   **S** 15 more times   **L** 17 more times
- Side 1 (instep) of each sock still has   **S** 32 sts   **L** 36 sts
- Side 2 (sole) of each sock now has   **S** 64 sts   **L** 72 sts

Shaping the Heel Cup, Sock B

Set Up This is a partial round, worked only on side 1 (instep) of both socks.
- **SIDE 1 (INSTEP), socks A and B:** Work the Peppercorn Chart as established.
- **ROTATE:** Rotate work and arrange stitches so that you are ready to begin working the heel on side 2 of sock B.

NOTE While shaping the heel cup and working the heel flap, you temporarily switch to working the socks individually. You first work side 2 of sock B back and forth in short rows, then you work side 2 of sock A in a similar manner. When the heels are completed, you return to knitting the socks together in rounds (in the Knitting the Legs section below). For information about short rows and wrapping stitches, see Tips for Shaping the Heel (page 34).

Side 2, Row 1 (right side)
- Knit   Ⓢ 16 sts   Ⓛ 18 sts
- Place marker 1.
- Knit   Ⓢ 31 sts   Ⓛ 35 sts
- Slip 1 as if to purl, bring yarn to the right side to wrap stitch, place marker 2 on left-hand needle, slip stitch back to left-hand needle. Turn work to the wrong side.

Side 2, Row 2 (wrong side) Purl to 1 stitch before marker 1, slip 1 as if to purl, bring yarn to right side to wrap stitch, slip stitch back to left-hand needle. Turn work to the right side.

Side 2, Row 3 (right side) Knit to 2 stitches before previously wrapped stitch, slip 1 as if to purl, bring yarn to right side to wrap stitch, slip stitch back to left-hand needle. Turn.

Side 2, Row 4 (wrong side) Purl to 2 stitches before previously wrapped stitch, slip 1 as if to purl, bring yarn to right side to wrap stitch, slip stitch back to left-hand needle. Turn.

Next Rows Repeat Rows 3 and 4 until all but the 4 center stitches have been wrapped. End having just completed Row 3.

Working the Heel Flap, Sock B

NOTE Continue to work back and forth in rows on side 2, sock B only. During the first two rows of the heel flap, you will be lifting and working the wraps that you created in the heel-cup shaping steps above. For information on lifting and working wraps on the right and wrong side, see Tips for Working Wrapped Stitches (page 38).

Side 2, Row 1 (wrong side) Purl, lifting the wraps and purling them together with their respective stitches as you come to them, to 1 stitch before marker 1. Then, lift the wrap of the stitch before marker 1, slip both stitch and wrap to the right-hand needle as if to purl, remove marker, slip both stitch and wrap back to the left-hand needle, and purl together the wrap and its stitch along with the next stitch (P3tog). Turn.

Side 2, Row 2 (right side) Slip 1 as if to purl. Then knit, lifting the wraps and knitting them together with their respective stitches as you come to them, to 1 stitch before marker 2. Lift the wrap of the next stitch completely over and to the left of the stitch, slip the stitch as if to knit, slip the wrap as if to knit, remove marker, slip next stitch as if to knit, place the 2 slipped stitches and the wrap back on left-hand needle, and knit the 2 slipped stitches together with the wrap through the back loop. Turn.

Side 2, Row 3 (wrong side) Slip 1 as if to purl, purl to 1 stitch before gap, P2tog to close gap. Turn.

NOTE From this point on, this heel flap is worked in Eye-of-Partridge Stitch (as written out in Rows 4–7) with a 2-stitch garter-stitch border and 1 edge stitch on each side.

Side 2, Row 4 (right side) Slip 1 as if to purl, K2, *slip 1, K1; repeat from * to 3 stitches before gap, K2, ssk to close gap. Turn.

Side 2, Row 5 (wrong side) Slip 1 as if to purl, K2, purl to 3 stitches before gap, K2, P2tog to close gap. Turn.

Side 2, Row 6 (right side) Slip 1 as if to purl, K2, *K1, slip 1; repeat from * to 3 stitches before gap, K2, ssk to close gap. Turn.

Side 2, Row 7 (wrong side) Slip 1 as if to purl, K2, purl to 3 stitches before gap, K2, P2tog to close gap. Turn.

Next Rows Repeat Rows 4–7 until you have decreased away all of the gusset stitches on side 2 of this sock. End having completed a right-side row.

• Side 2 of sock B now again has   S 32 sts   L 36 sts

Shaping the Heel Cup and Working the Heel Flap, Sock A

To shape the heel cup and work the heel flap of sock A, repeat the instructions for sock B above.

Knitting the Legs

In this section you return to working in the round on all stitches for both socks.

NOTE Pick up an extra stitch at the point where the heel and instep meet to prevent holes from developing. (See Knitting the Legs, pages 41–42.)

Next 4 Rounds Work all stitches in garter stitch beginning with a purl round.

Next 8 Rounds Work K1, P1 ribbing on all stitches.

Next 4 Rounds Work all stitches in garter stitch beginning with a purl round.

Next Rounds Continuing in the round, work on all stitches according to the Peppercorn Chart until the measurement from the top of the heel flap is approximately
                    Ⓢ 2¼" (5.5 cm)   Ⓛ 2¾" (7 cm)

Next 4 Rounds Work in garter stitch, beginning with a purl round.

Next 8 Rounds Work in K1, P1 ribbing on all stitches.

Next 4 Rounds Work all stitches in garter stitch, beginning with a purl round.

Finishing

Loosely bind off all stitches using your preferred method (see Bind Offs, pages 159–160). Weave in loose tails. Block.

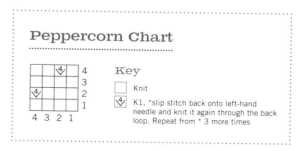

Peppercorn Chart

Key

☐ Knit

⩔ K1, *slip stitch back onto left-hand needle and knit it again through the back loop. Repeat from * 3 more times

Helix

I love stitches that move across surfaces, and they seem to find their way into many things that I do. Adding a bit of openwork to a cabled pattern is a big favorite. The juxtaposition of a solid, strong cable with open, gentle lace appeals to me aesthetically. Louet Gems is the perfect yarn for showing cables to their best advantage, and these socks definitely prove it. These socks are quite lovely and will be a striking addition to any wardrobe!

WOMAN'S SIZES	SMALL	LARGE
FINISHED FOOT CIRCUMFERENCE	7¼" (18.5 cm)	8" (20 cm)
YARN	Louet Gems Merino Fingering Weight (Superfine #1), 100% Merino wool, 1.75 oz (50g)/185 yds (169 m) [*Yarn-band gauge: 6.5–7.5 stitches = 1" (2.5 cm) on US 2–3 (2.75–3.25 mm) needles*]; Willow: 2 skeins for Small; 3 skeins for Large	
GAUGE	8 stitches and 11 rows = 1" (2.5 cm) in stockinette stitch	
NEEDLE	US 2 (2.75 mm) 40" (100 cm) circular, *or size needed to obtain correct gauge*	
NOTIONS	3 stitch markers (including 1 locking stitch marker), cable needle, darning needle	

Pattern Stitches

Stockinette
Knit every round.

Helix
See the Helix Charts on page 157.

Picot Edge
*K2, yo, K2tog; repeat from *.

⑤ Small   ⓛ Large

Casting On and Shaping the Toes

Cast On Follow the instructions for casting on stitches on pages 23–26 to cast on 16 stitches for sock B and 16 stitches for sock A.

Round 1 Follow the instructions for knitting Round 1 on pages 27–30 to knit the first round on both socks. You now have 8 stitches on side 1 (instep) for each sock and 8 stitches on side 2 (sole) for each sock.

Round 2 (increase)

NOTE All make 1 (M1) increases should be worked with a backward loop increase (see Backward Loop Increases on page 159).

- **SIDE 1 (INSTEP), sock A:** K1, M1R, knit to 1 stitch before the end, M1L, K1.
- **SIDE 1 (INSTEP), sock B:** K1, M1R, knit to 1 stitch before the end, M1L, K1.
- **ROTATE:** Rotate your work and arrange your stitches on the needles so that you are ready to work the sole stitches on side 2 of both socks.
- **SIDE 2 (SOLE), socks B and A:** Repeat the side 1 increases on both socks.
- Each sock now has 20 stitches (10 on each side of each sock).
- **ROTATE:** Rotate your work and arrange stitches so that you are ready to begin the next round.

Next Rounds
- Work Round 2 increases   ⑤ 5 more times   ⓛ 6 more times
- Each sock now has   ⑤ 40 sts   ⓛ 44 sts

Next Round (even) Knit both sides of socks A and B with no increases.

Next Round (increase) Repeat Round 2.

Next Rounds
- Repeat the last 2 rounds (knit even and increase)
                                   ⑤ 5 more times   ⓛ 6 more times
- End your work back at the marker having just finished side 2, sock A.
- Each sock now has a total of   ⑤ 64 sts   ⓛ 72 sts
- Each side of each sock now has   ⑤ 32 sts   ⓛ 36 sts

Ⓢ Small   Ⓛ Large

Knitting the Feet

Round 1

- **SIDE 1 (INSTEP), socks A and B:** Work the Helix Chart, beginning at the lower right.
- **SIDE 2 (SOLE), socks B and A:** Knit to end (stockinette stitch).

Next Rounds Repeat the previous round, continuing to work the Helix Chart on side 1 of each sock and keeping side 2 in stockinette stitch, until the socks measure the appropriate length (see Toe-to-Gusset Length, above). End your work having just finished side 2, sock A. You are back at your marker to begin the gusset increases.

TOE-TO-GUSSET LENGTH

Use this handy formula. Note: For Z, measure on side 2 of sock.

X	(desired total sock length)	= _____ "
Y	(# of rows in gusset and heel cup)	= 47 (S); 53 (L)
Z	(rows per inch)	= _____
TGL	(toe-to-gusset length)	= _____ "

$$\underset{X}{\underline{\quad\quad}}" - (\underset{Y}{\underline{\quad\quad}} \div \underset{Z}{\underline{\quad\quad}}) = \underset{TGL}{\underline{\quad\quad}}"$$

For more information, see Toe-Up Math, page 19.

Increasing for the Gussets

Round 1 (increase)

- **SIDE 1 (INSTEP), socks A and B:** Continue to work the Helix Chart as established.
- **SIDE 2 (SOLE), socks B and A:** K1, M1R, knit to last stitch of each sock, M1L, K1.

Round 2 (even)

- **SIDE 1 (INSTEP), socks A and B:** Continue to work the Helix Chart as established.
- **SIDE 2 (SOLE), socks B and A:** Work in stockinette stitch as established.

Next Rounds

- Repeat Rounds 1 and 2   Ⓢ 15 more times   Ⓛ 17 more times
- Side 1 (instep) of each sock still has   Ⓢ 32 sts   Ⓛ 36 sts
- Side 2 (sole) of each sock now has   Ⓢ 64 sts   Ⓛ 72 sts

Shaping the Heel Cup, Sock B

Set Up This is a partial round, worked only on side 1 (instep) of both socks.

- **SIDE 1** (INSTEP), **socks A and B:** Work the Helix Chart as established.
- **ROTATE:** Rotate work and arrange stitches so that you are ready to begin working the heel on side 2 of sock B.

NOTE While shaping the heel cup and working the heel flap, you temporarily switch to working the socks individually. You first work side 2 of sock B back and forth in short rows, then you work side 2 of Sock A in a similar manner. When the heels are completed, you return to knitting the socks together in rounds (in the Knitting the Legs section below). For information about short rows and wrapping stitches, see Tips for Shaping the Heel (page 34).

Side 2, Row 1 (right side)

- Knit   **S** 16 sts   **L** 18 sts
- Place marker 1.
- Knit   **S** 31 sts   **L** 35 sts
- Slip 1 as if to purl, bring yarn to the right side to wrap stitch, place marker 2 on left-hand needle, slip stitch back to left-hand needle. Turn work to the wrong side.

Side 2, Row 2 (wrong side) Purl to 1 stitch before marker 1, slip 1 as if to purl, bring yarn to right side to wrap stitch, slip stitch back to left-hand needle. Turn work to the right side.

Side 2, Row 3 (right side) Knit to 2 stitches before previously wrapped stitch, slip 1 as if to purl, bring yarn to right side to wrap stitch, slip stitch back to left-hand needle. Turn.

Side 2, Row 4 (wrong side) Purl to 2 stitches before previously wrapped stitch, slip 1 as if to purl, bring yarn to right side to wrap stitch, slip stitch back to left-hand needle. Turn.

Next Rows Repeat Rows 3 and 4 until all but the 4 center stitches have been wrapped. End having just completed Row 3.

Working the Heel Flap, Sock B

NOTE Continue to work back and forth in rows on side 2, sock B only. During the first two rows of the heel flap, you will be lifting and working the wraps that you created in the heel-cup shaping steps above. For information on lifting and working wraps on the right and wrong side, see Tips for Working Wrapped Stitches (page 38).

Side 2, Row 1 (wrong side) Purl, lifting the wraps and purling them together with their respective stitches as you come to them, to 1 stitch before marker 1. Then, lift the wrap of the stitch before marker 1, slip both stitch and wrap to the right-hand needle as if to purl, remove marker, slip both stitch and wrap back to the left-hand needle, and purl together the wrap and its stitch along with the next stitch (P3tog). Turn.

Side 2, Row 2 (right side) Slip 1 as if to purl. Then knit, lifting the wraps and knitting them together with their respective stitches as you come to them, to 1 stitch before marker 2. Lift the wrap of the next stitch completely over and to the left of the stitch, slip the stitch as if to knit, slip the wrap as if to knit, remove marker, slip next stitch as if to knit, place the 2 slipped stitches and the wrap back on left-hand needle, and knit the 2 slipped stitches together with the wrap through the back loop. Turn.

Side 2, Row 3 (wrong side) Slip 1 as if to purl, purl to 1 stitch before gap, P2tog to close gap. Turn.

NOTE From this point on, this heel flap is worked in Eye-of-Partridge Stitch (as written out in Rows 4–7) with a 2-stitch garter-stitch border and 1 edge stitch on each side.

Side 2, Row 4 (right side) Slip 1 as if to purl, K2, *slip 1, K1; repeat from * to 3 stitches before gap, K2, ssk to close gap. Turn.

Side 2, Row 5 (wrong side) Slip 1 as if to purl, K2, purl to 3 stitches before gap, K2, P2tog to close gap. Turn.

Side 2, Row 6 (right side) Slip 1 as if to purl, K2, *K1, slip 1; repeat from * to 3 stitches before gap, K2, ssk to close gap. Turn.

Side 2, Row 7 (wrong side) Slip 1 as if to purl, K2, purl to 3 stitches before gap, K2, P2tog to close gap. Turn.

Next Rows Repeat Rows 4–7 until you have decreased away all of the gusset stitches on side 2 of this sock. End having completed a right-side row.
  • Side 2 of sock B now again has   S 32 sts   L 36 sts

Shaping the Heel Cup and Working the Heel Flap, Sock A

To shape the heel cup and work the heel flap of sock A, repeat the instructions for sock B above.

Knitting the Legs

In this section you return to working in the round on all stitches for both socks.

NOTE Pick up an extra stitch at the point where the heel and instep meet to prevent holes from developing. (See Knitting the Legs, pages 41–42.)

Next Round
- SIDE 1 (INSTEP), **socks A and B:** Work across instep stitches according to the Helix Chart as established.
- SIDE 2 (SOLE), **socks B and A:** Work these stitches according to the Helix Chart, following the same row in the chart that you used on side 1.

Next Rounds Continue working in the round, following the Helix Chart for all stitches, until the leg measurement from the top of the heel flap is

S 6" (15 cm)   **L** 6½" (17 cm)

Next 4 Rounds Work in stockinette stitch on all stitches.

Next Round Work 1 round of Picot Edge on all stitches of both socks.

Next 4 Rounds Work stockinette stitch on all stitches.

Finishing

Loosely bind off all stitches using your preferred method (see Bind Offs, pages 159–160).

Turn the last 4 rounds to wrong side along the picot edge; stitch the bound-off edge loosely to the inside of the sock to create a hem. Sewing down the hem too firmly will cause the edge to lose its elasticity, and the sock may be difficult to put on.

Weave in any loose tails. Block.

Helix Chart for Size Small

12
11
10
9
8
7
6
5
4
3
2
1

32 31 30 29 28 27 26 25 24 23 22 21 20 19 18 17 16 15 14 13 12 11 10 9 8 7 6 5 4 3 2 1

Key

☐ Knit

• Purl

O Yarn over

⟋ Purl 2 together

Slip 2 to cable needle and hold in front, K2, K2 from cable needle

Right Twist. Slip 1 to cable needle and hold in back, K1, K1 from cable needle

Left Twist. Slip 1 to cable needle and hold in front, K1, K1 from cable needle

Helix Chart for Size Large

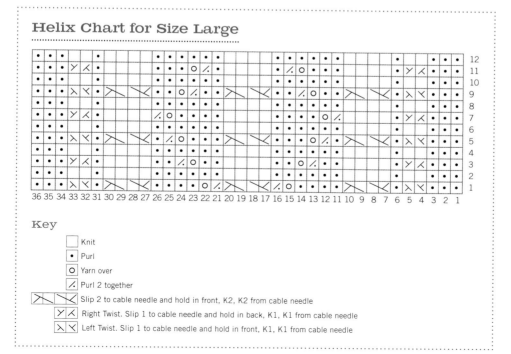

12
11
10
9
8
7
6
5
4
3
2
1

36 35 34 33 32 31 30 29 28 27 26 25 24 23 22 21 20 19 18 17 16 15 14 13 12 11 10 9 8 7 6 5 4 3 2 1

Key

☐ Knit

• Purl

O Yarn over

⟋ Purl 2 together

Slip 2 to cable needle and hold in front, K2, K2 from cable needle

Right Twist. Slip 1 to cable needle and hold in back, K1, K1 from cable needle

Left Twist. Slip 1 to cable needle and hold in front, K1, K1 from cable needle

Abbreviations

K	knit
K2tog	knit 2 stitches together
K3tog	knit 3 stitches together
Ktbl	knit through the back loop
M1L	make 1 stitch using left-leaning backward loop cast on
M1R	make 1 stitch using right-leaning backward loop cast on
P	purl
P2tog	purl 2 stitches together
ssk	slip, slip, knit
wyib	with yarn in back
yo	yarn over

Glossary

Decreases

Slip, slip, knit (ssk)

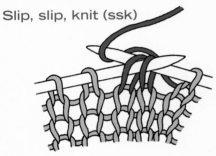

Slip two stitches, one at a time, as if to knit from the left-hand needle to the right-hand needle. Insert left-hand needle into the two slipped stitches from left to right, and knit them together.

Knit two together (K2tog)

Insert the right-hand needle into the next two stitches on the left-hand needle as if to knit, and knit them together.

Purl two together (P2tog)

Insert the right-hand needle into the next two stitches on the left-hand needle purlwise and purl them together.

Increases

Backward Loop Increases (M1)

For a left-leaning backward loop increase (M1L), make a backward loop onto the right needle so that the working yarn points away from you.

For a right-leaning backward loop increase (M1R), make a backward loop onto the right needle so that the working yarn points toward you.

Yarn over (yo)

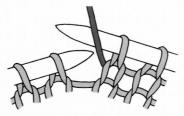

Bring the working yarn to the front between the two needles. Take the working yarn over the right-hand needle to the back to make your next stitch.

Bind Offs

For more information, see Binding Off on page 13.

Basic Bind Off

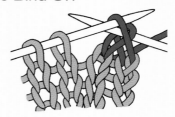

Knit the first two stitches. *Insert the point of your left-hand needle into the first stitch on the right-hand needle, and lift this stitch over the second stitch and off the needle. Knit another stitch, and repeat from *.

Sewn Bind Off

A

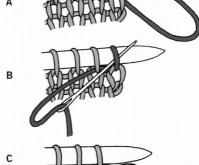
B

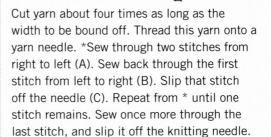
C

Cut yarn about four times as long as the width to be bound off. Thread this yarn onto a yarn needle. *Sew through two stitches from right to left (A). Sew back through the first stitch from left to right (B). Slip that stitch off the needle (C). Repeat from * until one stitch remains. Sew once more through the last stitch, and slip it off the knitting needle.

Tubular Bind Off

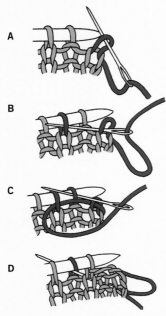

Cut yarn, leaving a tail about four times as long as the width to be bound off, and thread it onto a yarn needle. *Insert the tip of the sewing needle as if to knit into the first stitch and slip it off the knitting needle (A). Insert the yarn needle into the third stitch as if to purl and pull the yarn through (B). Insert the yarn needle as if to purl into the second stitch and slide it off the knitting needle (C). Bring the yarn and yarn needle to the back of the work and insert the yarn needle as if to knit into the fourth stitch, pulling the yarn through (D). Note that two stitches have been dropped off the knitting needle and two others have been worked but remain on the knitting needle. These two stitches will be the first and second stitches as you work through each step of the instructions again. Repeat from * until all stitches have been worked.

Other Techniques and Terms

"As if to knit" or knitwise (kwise)

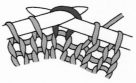

When a pattern says "slip the next stitch as if to knit" or "slip the next stitch knitwise," insert your needle into the next stitch from front to back as if you were going to knit it, then slip it to the right-hand needle without knitting it.

"As if to purl" or purlwise (pwise)

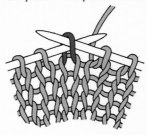

When a pattern says "slip the next stitch as if to purl" or "slip the next stitch purlwise," insert your needle into the next stitch from back to front as if you were going to purl it, then slip it to the right-hand needle without purling it.

Blocking

Most of the time when I complete a pair of socks, they move off the needles and onto my family's feet without a moment's thought. For gift giving, however, I do block. To block finished socks, first soak them in warm water and a no-rinse wool wash such as Eucalan. Squeeze to remove the excess water. Place them in an empty washing machine and run one *spin only* cycle. A great low-cost, low-energy alternative to this is a salad spinner; I like OXO's large capacity model. Once you've spun the socks, remove them from the washing machine or spinner and place them on sock blockers to dry. Fiber Trends offers these in a variety of sizes, but you can also make your own out of old wire coat hangers bent into the shape and size of a foot. Allow the socks to dry completely before removing the blocker.

Knit through the back loop (Ktbl)

Insert the right-hand needle into the part of the next stitch that lies behind the left-hand needle and work from that position.

Stranding

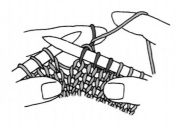

Working with more than one color while knitting is not difficult if you follow a couple of basic rules. Do not carry your yarn for more than three stitches without twisting the colors on the wrong side of the work.

Carrying your yarn across more than three stitches results in long floats that catch fingers and toes, and can cause stitch distortion on the right side of your work. For contrasting colors used in short sections, I generally use yarn bobbins. These can be purchased or hand-cut from scraps of thin cardboard. If you have never worked with color before, try stranding on a swatch using both one- and two-handed techniques to determine which gives you more consistent tension on all stitches.

Weaving in the ends

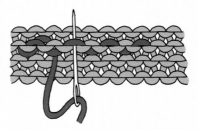

When your project is complete, you are left with yarn "tails." First take the tail ends to the wrong side of your fabric, threading them onto a darning needle to draw them through. Using the darning needle, weave each tail, one at a time, across the wrong side of the fabric, under the purl bumps of the stitches. A general rule of thumb is to weave each yarn tail across a minimum of four stitches and change directions at least three times. Once you have woven in the yarn, use your fingers to gently tug and stretch the fabric a bit to even the tension, then clip the yarn end close to the work.

Working Wrapped Stitches

For more information, see Tips for Working Wrapped Stitches on page 38.

Lifting and knitting a wrap on the right side

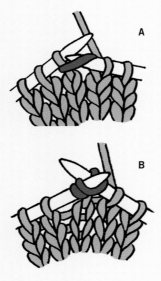

Insert the tip of the right-hand needle under the near side of the wrap. Lift the wrap straight up and onto the left-hand needle (A). The wrap will cross over the stitch to form an X-shape, with the top of the wrap to the right of the top of the stitch. Knit the stitch and wrap together by inserting the right needle between the bottom legs of this X and then straight back so the needle goes between the 2 vertical strands behind the needle (B). It's important to be certain that you've knitted into the middle of the wrap loop just as you would any stitch.

Lifting and purling a wrap on the wrong side

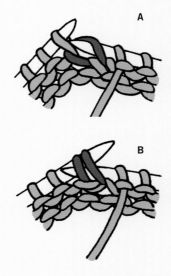

Insert the tip of the right-hand needle under the far side of the wrap and lift it onto the left needle (A). Then purl together the wrap and its stitch (B).

Resources

Blue Moon Fiber Arts
info@bluemoonfiberarts.com
www.bluemoonfiberarts.com
Socks That Rock

Clover-USA
800-233-1703
www.clover-usa.com
Chibi tapestry needles,
locking stitch markers, yarn
bobbins

Dream In Color
Available online from:
The Loopy Ewe
www.theloopyewe.com

Green Mountain Spinnery
800-321-9665
www.spinnery.com
Cotton Comfort

Knit One, Crochet Too
800-357-7646
www.knitonecrochettoo.com
Ty-Dy Socks

Knit Picks
800-574-1323
www.knitpicks.com
Stroll Tweed, Harmony fixed
circular needles

Kollage Yarns
541-929-2359
www.kollageneedleshop.com
Kollage Yarns Square
Circular needles

Kraemer Yarns
800-759-5601
www.kraemeryarns.com
Sterling Silk & Silver

Lantern Moon
800-530-4170
www.lanternmoon.com
Destiny Needles

Lorna's Laces
773-935-3803
www.lornaslaces.net
Shepherd Sock

Louet North America
800-897-6444
www.louet.com
Louet Gems Merino

Malabrigo
786-427-1048
www.malabrigoyarn.com
Malabrigo Sock

Noro
Distributed exclusively in
the United States by:
K. F. I.
*knittingfever@
    knittingfever.com*
www.knittingfever.com
Silk Garden Sock

Inox
Circular needles
available from:
WEBS
800-367-9327
www.yarn.com

Skacel Collection, Inc.
800-255-1278
www.skacelknitting.com
Addi Natura, Turbo, and
Lace needles

Valley Fibers/WEBS
800-367-9327
www.yarn.com
Valley Yarns Huntington,
Valley Yarns Franklin, Valley
Yarns Valley Superwash

YLI Corporation
803-985-3100
www.ylicorp.com
Woolly Nylon thread

Standard Sock Sizes

The sizes given with each sock pattern indicate the number of inches or centimeters in circumference. Here, you can find standard lengths, corresponding to U.S. shoe sizes.

Women

SHOE SIZE	LENGTH IN INCHES	LENGTH IN CENTIMETERS
3	8	20.25
3.5	8.12	20.75
4	8.33	21.25
4.5	8.5	21.5
5	8.67	22
5.5	8.88	22.5
6	9	22.75
6.5	9.17	23.25
7	9.38	23.75
7.5	9.5	24
8	9.62	24.5
8.5	9.75	24.75
9	10	25.5
9.5	10.25	26
10	10.33	26.25
10.5	10.5	26.75
11	10.67	27
11.5	10.88	27.5
12	11	28
12.5	11.17	28.25

Men

SHOE SIZE	LENGTH IN INCHES	LENGTH IN CENTIMETERS
5	9	22.75
5.5	9.17	23.25
6	9.38	23.75
6.5	9.5	24
7	9.62	24.5
7.5	9.75	24.75
8	10	25.5
8.5	10.25	26
9	10.33	26.25
9.5	10.5	26.75
10	10.67	27
10.5	10.88	27.5
11	11	28
11.5	11.17	28.25
12	11.38	29
12.5	11.5	29.25
13	11.67	29.75
13.5	11.88	30.25
14	12	30.5
14.5	12.12	30.75
15	12.38	31.5

Children

SHOE SIZE	LENGTH IN INCHES	LENGTH IN CENTIMETERS	SHOE SIZE	LENGTH IN INCHES	LENGTH IN CENTIMETERS
1	3.33	8.5	10	6.5	16.5
1.5	3.5	9	10.5	6.62	16.75
2	3.67	9.25	11	5 6.75	17.25
2.5	3.88	9.75	11.5	7	17.75
3	4	10	12	7.12	18
3.5	4.17	10.5	12.5	7.25	18.5
4	4.38	11	13	7.38	18.75
4.5	4.62	11.75	13.5	7.5	19
5	4.75	12	1	7.75	19.75
5.5	4.88	12.25	1.5	7.88	20
6	5.12	13	2	8.12	20.75
6.5	5.25	13.25	2.5	8.33	21.25
7	5.38	13.75	3	8.5	21.5
7.5	5.5	14	3.5	8.62	22
8	5.75	14.5	4	8.75	22.25
8.5	5.88	15	4.5	9	22.75
9	6.12	15.5	5	9.25	23.5
9.5	6.25	16			

Acknowledgments

No one lives or works in a vacuum. This book would not exist without the help of some very important people.

My first thanks go to God, who gave me what I needed to get this done. This book bumped right into my personal life in a manner that required me to get very creative in order to have it all done on time. I could never have done it on my own.

I owe more than I can ever repay to my husband Gene, who puts up with so much from me, sometimes the least of which is my desire to pursue this yarn-filled dream instead of settling down and getting a "real job" like the other grown-ups. Mr. Wonderful, you are truly a man among men, and I cannot ever give back to you what you've given to me. In all ways you've allowed me the freedom to be who I really am, sacrificing so that I could figure out who that is. I am so grateful to you, more than I can ever express.

I must also say a very special thank you to Kathy Elkins, Mary Kubasek-Haber, Kristen Gonsalves, Rue Shanti, Mary-Alice Baker, Clara Parkes, Tina Newton, Linda Roghaar, and Cat Bordhi. Your encouragement and assistance helped me through a couple of rough spots at times along this journey. On a few choice days, when for various reasons I didn't think it would happen, you each gave me words that kept me going. Thank you!

Many thanks to Storey Publishing for giving me another opportunity to share my work with knitters around the world. Special thanks to Kathy Brock and Tamara Stone-Snyder; making sure my ideas work is not the easiest job in the world, and I always appreciate every challenge you offer me.

To my sample knitters and friends, many, many thanks. These women do more than knit socks. They offer exceptional feedback on technique and patterns, emotional support, and occasionally, crisis intervention, which often involves things like wine, Brie, chocolate, and people to share it with. They are always willing to sacrifice for the cause. Mary-Alice Baker, Gail Callahan, Dena Childs, Barb Giguere, Kristen Gonsalves, Mary Kubasek-Haber, Rue Shanti, Tamara Stone-Snyder, Katy Wight — thank you so very much. I said it before and shall say it again: This couldn't happen without you. And once again, we party!

Index

Page numbers in *italics* indicate photographs or illustrations. Page numbers in **bold** indicate charts or tables.

Take Your Knitting to the Next Level with More Storey Books

by Judith Durant

Make your knitting pop with these 94 braids, diamonds, pretzels, circles, reversible cables, and more. In-depth instructions and close-up photos will demystify the technique and offer a bounty of design inspiration.

by Leslie Ann Bestor

This one-of-a-kind reference for more than 50 ways to cast on and bind off features step-by-step photography and detailed instructions to ensure that all your knitting projects get the perfect beginning and ending.

by Lea Redmond

Use your knitting needles to record the beauty and emotions of your everyday experiences! More than 30 enchanting projects, accompanied by whimsical illustrations, will inspire you to expand your creativity as you observe and explore the world.

by Margaret Radcliffe

Knitters of all levels will find solutions to their knitting problems in this essential reference. The easy-to-use Q & A format covers everything from casting on and binding off to reading patterns, managing multiple colors, finishing, and more.

edited by Judith Durant

Use your orphan skeins to make delightful one-of-a-kind projects. Here are 101 patterns for baby clothes, mittens, scarves, shawls, hats, bags, toys, and of course, socks!

Join the conversation. Share your experience with this book, learn more about Storey Publishing's authors, and read original essays and book excerpts at storey.com. Look for our books wherever quality books are sold or by calling 800-441-5700.